Garden
crafts

Garden crafts

30 Beautiful and Practical Projects for Patio, Porch, Deck, Garden, or Yard

Elizabeth C. Letcavage

STACKPOLE
BOOKS

Copyright © 2015 by Stackpole Books

Published by
STACKPOLE BOOKS
5067 Ritter Road
Mechanicsburg, PA 17055
www.stackpolebooks.com

Printed in the United States of America

10 9 8 7 6 5 4 3 2 1

First edition

Cover design by Tessa Sweigert
Cover image by Alan Wycheck
Photos by Alan Wycheck except where noted

Library of Congress Cataloging-in-Publication Data

Letcavage, Elizabeth.
  Garden crafts : 30 beautiful and practical projects for patio, porch, deck, garden, or yard / Elizabeth C. Letcavage. — First edition.
       pages cm
  Includes index.
  ISBN 978-0-8117-1303-0
  1. Garden ornaments and furniture. 2. Handicraft. I. Title.
   SB473.5.L47 2015
   745.5—dc23
                                          2014040647

Contents

Introduction

Gardening and crafting are high on my list of passions in life, and I suspect there are many like-minded people who share these two hobbies. We all find pleasure in transforming a pile of stuff into something beautiful and often useful. Many of the projects in this book offer opportunities to recycle, repurpose, and reuse items that would otherwise go to the landfill. And gardeners will appreciate that deer, rabbits, groundhogs, and other critters will not eat them!

These craft projects require a wide range of materials. While I list particular brands that worked well, there are a host of suitable substitutes. Every crafter has favorite brands of materials and tools, so use what you are accustomed to and have on hand.

Design and color use are also matters of personal preference. There are infinite ways to express yourself with these garden projects. I hope that you will be inspired to make each project your own.

Like ephemeral spring flowers, all craft projects will fade and deteriorate over time if exposed to the elements. They may not be family heirlooms, but I hope you will enjoy your handcrafted artwork and your garden for many seasons to come.

Happy crafting!

Equipment
& supplies

Safety Gear

The most important equipment you will need before starting any project is protective gear. Safety glasses are a must anytime you work with hammers, saws, drills, sanders, and dusty materials. Gloves are often a personal choice; however, the occasions where they are highly recommended are noted in the instructions. A dust mask is only called for when projects involve concrete, mortar, or grout, but you may also want to wear one when sanding. Please stay safe and use your gear.

Vise

Often materials need to be held down for cutting or assembling. If you don't own a workbench vise, consider investing in a lightweight, portable work station, which can be moved to your preferred work site, indoors or out. Top with a piece of plywood and you have a small workbench.

Measuring and Marking Tools

The old carpenter's saying, "Measure twice, cut once," is good advice for crafters, too. A metal yardstick and 10' metal tape measure are good investments. A flexible seamstress tape is required to measure curved or round objects. A carpenter's triangle is handy, but not necessary. You'll also need a handful of sharpened pencils and a fine-tipped permanent marker. Even though the projects in this book provide marking and cutting measurements, you will want to calculate them using your project materials.

1

Adhesives

The many great adhesives on the market today serve every purpose imaginable. The project instructions will specify which glues to use, but you may be able to substitute in many cases. Check the product's packaging for a list of materials the glue will adhere. For these outdoor projects, heavy duty construction adhesive, applied with an inexpensive caulking gun, is a go-to product. Another product you'll want to have on hand is clear silicone tub and tile sealant, which is sold in a resealable tube. White glues (PVA type) and yellow (wood) glues are used routinely. Select those that are water resistant or waterproof. Specialty glues, such as CPVA, fabric, super-type and permanent rubber-based epoxy, are also used in some of the projects.

Surface Protectors

Stock up on tarps, drop cloths, old towels, and plastic sheeting. Almost every craft project in the book requires tabletop or workbench protection.

Tools

Roy Underhill is still working at *The Woodwright's Shop* on PBS television making wonderful furniture the old-fashioned way with just hand tools. He proves it's possible, but for the modern crafter power tools offer a fast and accurate way to get things done. Here's a rundown of the tools used to make these garden crafts.

- The one essential tool is a battery-powered hand drill. (Opt for a combination drill/screwdriver if you are buying a new one.) You'll also need a set of the common size drill bits. A couple of projects require large drill bits and a spade (or butterfly) bit to make large holes. Borrowing these items may be a good option if you are only going to use them occasionally.
- A well-stocked crafter's tool bag will always include sharp scissors, a utility knife, and wire cutters. A hacksaw is used to cut metal pipe and rod, and a wood handsaw takes care of small jobs.
- Hammers and wrenches are staples in the household tool box, but you may not have chisels and clamps. These items are not used extensively, so you may choose to borrow these, as well. A tack hammer (a small version of a hammer) is used quite a bit for fastening more delicate pieces.
- A power hand sander is helpful, but if you don't have one, that's not a problem. Most of the projects are rustic and need only a light sanding to remove splinters and old paint. A small 2" x 4" scrap of wood can serve as a sanding block. (A rotary tool is recommended for making the watermelon slice punk holder; although hand sanding is possible, it will take some effort.)

Fasteners

The fastener used most often for outdoor projects in this book is a galvanized deck screw. They're strong and don't rust. Have plenty of these on hand. Finish nails and regular staples are also used in abundance. You may not be familiar with the U-shaped wire staples, but chances are you will find many other uses for them in your future crafting projects. Sizing for eye bolts and screws and S-hooks is specified with each project and these may be purchased individually or in bulk packs at hardware stores.

Hangers

Before you buy wire to hang or connect something, check around the house. Those who ardently repurpose things will have an adequate supply of wire on hand. Computer cables and old telephone cords will fill the bill in many cases. Chain is a bit pricey when sold by the foot, so check discount stores for prepackaged jack chain to save money. Heavy-weight monofilament can be used for more than just catching fish. It is strong and clear, so it does not compete for attention with the finished project.

Brushes

The sizes and types of brushes that are used for various purposes depend a lot on personal preference. Some products will specify whether a natural bristle or synthetic brush should be used. Plenty of disposable foam and chip brushes are used for projects in this book in those situations in which cleanup would be messy and time consuming. Use good-quality artist's brushes for all detailed finish painting and fine art work.

Paint

Bare wood and metal must have a base coat of primer paint, which helps the paint adhere to the object and offers an additional layer of protection. Priming coats are not required with some deck paints and stains, and some paint has the primer incorporated in it, so check the label of the product you are using for instructions.

- Leftover deck paint is used for many of the projects in this book because it does not require a primer coat, is very long lasting, and is economical. The dark, muted colors are perfect to give items a woodsy, organic feel.

- On the opposite end of the spectrum is outdoor enamel paint. Crafts painted in bright colors and high gloss finishes just seem to shout, "Look at me!" Outdoor enamels are extremely durable once they have cured. You can work with recently painted items that are dry to the touch, but they should be allowed to dry for several additional weeks before they are exposed to the elements.

- One of the most useful products for crafters is spray paint formulated for plastics. It can be used on everything (even though the label will tell you otherwise, it will adhere to galvanized metal), although it does call for a primer when used on bare wood or metal. It holds up well over time and the color selection is vast. When using any type of spray paint, be sure to shake the can for the full recommended time. When finished, always spray a few bursts with the can upside down to clear the nozzle. (If you do clog the nozzle, you may be able to salvage the contents by replacing the nozzle with one from another can that is exactly the same product.)

- You may be surprised to discover how versatile acrylic craft paint is. Bottles of craft acrylic paints are available in almost any color you would want and are very inexpensive. Colors are more limited with tubes of student grade or artist's grade acrylic, but they can be mixed to produce any color you need. The primary difference is that craft acrylic contains more water and less pigment.

Sealants

For maximum weather protection, most projects are finished with a seal coat. Clear aerosol acrylic, polyurethane, and spar varnish sealants are convenient and easy to use. Most products are available in satin or gloss finish, and will often require two coats for complete coverage. Although it is more expensive, acrylic seal coat with UV protection is worth the extra cost for its ability to protect colors from fading. Brush-on polyurethane and spar varnish are used for the ultimate in weather protection. Keep in mind that varnish and shellac will yellow over time, which may affect the appearance of your project.

Waterproofers

The two types of waterproofing materials used in this book are both made to seal concrete block. One is a white, latex-based paint that contains some grit, and the other is a clear, water-based acrylic product. Either one works well and can be used with acrylic or latex paints.

Stroll Down
the garden path

Geometric
wind spinner

A simple geometric shape made with plumbing pipe forms a changing display of interesting designs as the wind blows. You can make one of these in the morning and have it hanging on a tree branch or shepherd's hook to catch the afternoon breeze. Adults will enjoy these as much as kids.

EQUIPMENT

Drill with $^1/_{16}$" drill bit

Grooved locking pliers

Ratcheting pipe cutting tool or
hacksaw and vise

SUPPLIES

78" length of $^1/_2$" CPVC (chlorinated
polyvinyl chloride) pipe

$^1/_2$" CPVC elbows (12)

Can of CPVC glue

$^1/_4$" eye hook

#7 barrel swivel with interlock

Can of spray paint formulated for
plastics

Monofilament fishing line (to hang
the spinner)

Latex or rubber gloves

Permanent marker

Newspapers or table protector

Clean-up rag for glue

About CPVC Pipe

To a plumber or contractor, there are important differences between CPVC and PVC pipe, but for this project the only difference is aesthetics. Regular white PVC pipe and elbows are larger than CPVC ones, but may be used if you like the look. Keep in mind that the glue for CPVC and PVC differs, so be sure to select the one that matches your pipe. Hardware stores and plumbing suppliers typically carry CPVC and PVC pipe in 10' lengths. If the store will cut this in sections so that it fits in your vehicle, have it cut so that you have one 65" length and one 55" length. Two 10' pipes will yield three wind spinners.

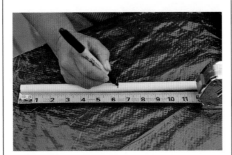

1. Using a permanent ink pen, make marks at $6^1/_2$" intervals along the length of the pipe(s).

2. If you are using a hacksaw, place the pipe in a vise for stability, and be sure your saw is perpendicular to the pipe when cutting. Cut the pipe at each mark, resulting in twelve sections, each $6^1/_2$" long.

3. If you happen to have a scissor-like ratcheting pipe cutter, the process will be speedy.

4. Use your fingers to remove any loose filings on the pipe ends.

5. Connect two pipe sections to one elbow. Make four sets.

6. Connect elbows to two sets of pipes, so that the elbows are facing straight up. These are the base units.

7. Attach pipes to the two base unit elbows. The elbows with pipes should be facing toward you.

8. Connect elbows to the remaining two sets of pipes. On the right arm of one set, place the elbow opening facing up at a 90 degree angle. On the left arm, place the elbow facing down at a 90 degree angle. On the other set, place the elbow opening facing down at a 90 degree angle on the right arm and facing up at a 90 degree angle on the left arm.

9. Place the left and right pipe sets next to one base unit, as shown, so that the pipes are at 90 degree angles.

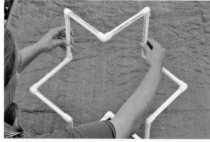

10. Lift the right set straight up and connect the elbow to the pipe. Repeat with the right side. Attach the remaining base unit to the two remaining elbow joints. Adjust so that all joints and pipes are at 90 degree angles.

11. Use the permanent marker to number the pipe and the matching elbow at each of the 24 joints, and to strike a line-up mark on the pipe and elbow. This will ensure that you don't forget to glue one of the joints, and that the pipes will be glued at the correct angle. This is an important step, as this glue dries very fast and forms a permanent bond.

12. Protect the table surface and put on gloves. Separate the pipe and elbow at joint #1. Unscrew the cap of CPVC glue—you may need to use grooved locking pliers to remove the cap for the first time—and swirl the brush around the can rim to remove excess glue.

13. Insert the brush all the way into the elbow, remove it quickly, and replace it in the can.

14. Without delay, insert the pipe into the elbow and quickly line up the marks. Allow to set for ten seconds before moving on to the next joint. If glue drips fall onto the outside of the pipes or elbow, wipe up immediately with the rag. Glue the remaining joints in the same manner.

15. With the permanent marker, place a dot in the center of one of the elbows. Drill a hole on the mark using a ¹/₆" drill bit. (Handyman's tip: If you insert small drill bits all the way into the chuck, you will be less likely to break the bit.)

16. Glue the pointed tip of a ¹/₄" eye hook.

17. Thread it into the hole and finger tighten.

18. Use pliers to screw in the eye hook until all threads are in the hole and the hook opening is perpendicular to the pipe.

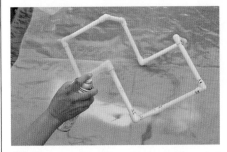

19. Spray paint the spinner with paint that is formulated for plastic. No primer coat is needed when using this paint, which is phenomenal in its ability to adhere to slick surfaces and endure harsh weather; however, two

coats are needed to adequately cover the numbers and strike lines. To get the most impact from this ornament, select a paint color that contrasts with its background from the primary viewing point. Bright primary colors really pop when placed in front of green tree and shrub foliage.

20. After the spinner has dried (which should take less than an hour), attach the barrel swivel to the screw eye. Cut a length of fishing line to accommodate your hanging site. Attach the monofilament to the swivel using a cinch knot.

To make a cinch knot, insert one end of the fishing line through the swivel and leave a 4" tail. Wrap the tail around the long line four or five times. Insert the tail end back through the swivel. Secure the tail by inserting into the loop closest to the swivel. Trim the end close to the swivel.

Gardeners of all ages will enjoy watching as the spinner forms a variety of interesting shapes.

Whimsy Sticks

This project makes good use of your creativity and supplies you may already have. Creative possibilities for this project abound. A whimsy stick may be decorative or practical. It may be fanciful or classy. It can be designed to enhance cottage gardens or formal gardens. To make a whimsy stick, some crafters will include odds and ends destined for the next yard sale or the landfill, while others will give a new purpose to various household or garden items. This eco-friendly project can help you celebrate any holiday theme or garden scheme.

EQUIPMENT

Work table with vise

Palm sander

Medium grit
  sandpaper (#220)

Hacksaw

Hammer

Screwdriver

Wire cutters

Drill with $1/8$" and
  $1/4$" bits and $1/2$"
  spade bit

Ruler or measuring
  tape

Pencil or permanent
  marker

$1^1/_2$" or 2" flat
  paintbrush

SUPPLIES

42" pressure-treated
  deck baluster that
  is mitered at one
  end

1 foot $1/4$" metal
  threaded or rolled
  round rod or reinforced
  construction bar (rebar) ($5/_{16}$" rod
  may be used, but you will need to
  use a corresponding drill bit to
  install it.)

#8 1" wood screw

$1^1/_2$" finish nails

$1/2$" wire (cable) staples

Metal or galvanized metal watering
  can

Purchased metal flower

Plastic male outdoor water faucet

Wood primer

Green outdoor enamel paint

Spray paint for metal or plastic—red,
  yellow, and orange

6' length of recycled garden hose

Rickrack used for sewing

Paper

Pencil

Circle template

Sheet of plain copy paper or card
  stock and sheet of tracing paper

About Materials

Whimsy sticks start with a sturdy deck baluster and a strong bar to secure it into the ground. Almost anything can be attached to your baluster using one of the three techniques that are illustrated. Gather up your odds and ends garden items and craft supplies. Check the junk drawer, garage, and workshop for unused items. Then let your creativity rip.

This tutorial features a mix of dollar store finds, hardware and recycled items to create a purely decorative stick. They may also serve practical purposes, such as the birdbath and lantern that are shown at the end. While the bird house whimsy may look practical at first glance, it is decorative for the reasons provided in the caption.

1. It is a good idea to wear gloves and safety glasses while preparing the stick. Sand the baluster to remove splintered wood, dirt, and oil spots with medium grit sandpaper (#220). You can opt for a palm sander or wrap a sheet of paper around a small 2" x 4" wood block.

2. Apply a coat of primer paint and allow it to dry. If you plan to use deck paint or stain, primer is usually not required. Check the instructions on the paint you are using.

3. Use a pencil or permanent marker to place a line at the 1' mark on the metal bar.

4. Secure the metal bar in the vise lengthwise. Use a hacksaw to cut off 12" of bar and set it aside.

5. Secure the baluster in the vise vertically, with the flat end facing upward.

6. On the flat end of the baluster, draw a line from one corner to the other. Repeat using the other two corners.

7. Mark the center of the "X" with the pencil or permanent marker. Drill a deep hole at the "X" with a bit that is slightly smaller than threaded or rolled bar. In this instance, the bar is $^3/_8$" and the drill bit used is $^5/_{16}$". Drill as far in as the bit will go.

8. Use a hammer to pound the metal bar into the hole. Keep the bar straight up and down as you pound

it as far in as you can, but no more than 6".

9. Paint the entire stick with green outdoor enamel (or your choice of paint). Let this dry and apply a second coat if necessary, following recommended drying times on the label. Enamel paints will dry to the touch in several hours, but it takes several days for them to completely cure. Until it is cured to a hard finish, the paint is susceptible to chipping.

10. Move on now to the watering can. If your watering can is rusty, sand the visible rust off for best results. Clean the can with soap and water prior to painting it, and apply a metal priming paint if the metal is bare. The first coat of spray paint applied will end up being the color of the flower petals.

11. To make a painting mask of a flower, draw or trace a flower petal from a coloring book on plain paper or card stock. Cut it out, use it as a pattern to trace four additional petals, and cut them out.

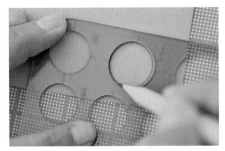

12. Use a template to draw a circle that will form the center disk of the flower.

13. Use white glue to attach the petals to the center disk.

14. Wrap a length of rickrack along the bottom edge and cut it to fit, allowing for a slight overlap. Do the same for the top rim.

15. Place the paper flower and rickrack on a protective surface and spray with adhesive.

16. Affix the rickrack to the can. Place the can on your work surface with the handle facing to the right. Position the flower in the center of the can and press down firmly on all edges.

17. Use painter's tape to mask off any area that you do not want to be sprayed with the second color of outdoor spray paint. Spray with a sweeping motion. Try not to angle the spray in a way that would force paint under the masked areas. Before removing the masking, decide if a second coat is needed. Follow label directions on recoating. The moisture in the spray paint may cause the paper pattern to pop off. Give the loose part a quick burst of spray glue if necessary. Allow the paint to dry thoroughly.

18. The paper pattern and the rickrack should pull off easily in one smooth motion. Clean off any glue residue with a paper towel soaked with rubbing alcohol.

19. In the center of a sheet of tracing paper, use a template to draw a circle that is slightly larger than the one you drew for the flower pattern mask. Carefully cut out the circle using a craft knife.

20. Position the center of the circle over the center of your painted flower. In this case, the weight of the paper was sufficient to hold down the sides of the tracing paper, but you may need to secure it with tape. Spray the flower center red (or the color of your choice). Remove the tracing paper after the paint gets tacky.

21. Use tape and newspapers to mask off the can so that you can spray a third color on the watering can head. The red paint used here will match the faucet handle.

22. Using a $^3/_{16}$" bit, drill a hole in the center of the bottom of the can. Drill another $^3/_{16}$" hole in the bottom, at the edge under the spout. This hole

will let rain water drain so that the can doesn't fill up.

23. Find the center of the top of your stick by drawing lines from corner to corner. Mark the center of the "X."

24. Drill a pilot hole about $^1/_4$" deep into the center of the stick with a drill bit sized to match your screw. In this case, a $^1/_8$" bit was used to match a #8 1" wood screw. Keep your drill perpendicular to the surface of the wood.

25. Place the screw in the center hole of the can and hold it with one hand while guiding it to the hole in the baluster with the other. Use a hand screwdriver to secure the screw into the wood.

26. On the longer side of the stick, make a mark where you would like your faucet to be placed. This one is $5^1/_2$" from the top.

27. Place the point of the ¹/₂" spade bit onto your mark. Drill a hole into the stick at a 90 degree angle, ³/₄" deep.

28. Screw the faucet into the hole until it is flush with the stick and the hose outlet is facing downward.

29. Screw the hose onto the faucet. The hose used for this project was

washed with soap and water and painted bright chartreuse with spray paint created for plastics. Note that it takes longer for paint to dry on the rubber surface.

30. Lay the stick on its side on a work table with the watering can extending over the table. Wrap the hose around the stick three or four times. Don't worry about placement at this time.

31. Position the first wrap close to the hose faucet and secure the hose to the stick using 1¹/₂" finish nails. Hammer the nail so it just goes through the top layer of hose. Nail the hose to the stick at the next twist and so on, spacing the hose evenly as you go. Nail the last bit of hose close to the end of the stick.

32. Cut off the excess hose about an inch longer than the stick.

33. Place the metal flower head directly below the watering can head.

34. Mark the angle where the wire stem crosses the stick.

35. Use a drill bit sized to match the metal wire stem to make an angled hole at the mark. Be sure not to drill through the hose. Push the stem wire through the hole until the flower is positioned properly.

36. Secure the stem to the stick with several 1/2" wire staples.

37. Bend up the excess wire where it meets the last staple and cut it off with wire cutters. Hammer down the end if necessary.

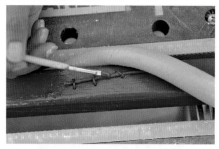

38. Paint the wire and staples.

Attaching Items with Magnets

In some cases, you will want to be able to remove the decorative items from the stick in order to clean them, store them or light them (as with the lantern whimsy shown at the end). This can be accomplished by attaching magnets to your decorative item and a square or round electrical box cover to the baluster.

1. To prevent the electrical box cover from spinning wildly as you drill a hole in the center, you will need to attach the plate to a wood block. Screw the plate onto the wood in the pre-drilled holes of the box. Use 1/2" wood screws or any that you have on hand that will do the job.

2. Mark the center of the plate with a pencil or permanent marker. Use a nail set to punch a dimple in the center of the metal plate. This will keep the drill bit from slipping off of the plate while you drill.

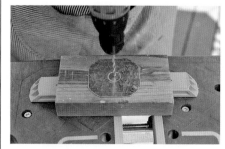

3. Position a 1/8" drill bit on top of the dimple and make a hole through the center of the plate.

4. Mark the center of the baluster as previously shown in step 22.

5. Screw the plate onto the baluster using a #8 1" wood screw.

6. Trace the outline of the electrical plate onto your decorative item—in this case, a hammered aluminum tray.

7. Use an appropriate adhesive that will attach magnets to whatever material your item is made of. Water resistant white glue was used to attach the magnets to the metal tray. Regular craft magnets were used for this birdbath top. If your decorative item is heavy or if the weight is not balanced, consider paying a bit more for super or "rare earth" magnets that have more holding power and use super-type glue.

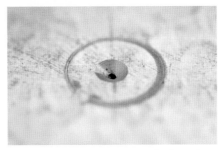

8. If the plate needs to sit flush with your item, countersink the screw so it sits into the screw hole and flush with the plate. Use a drill bit to make a depression in the metal that is the size of the screw head you will be using. Then, make the hole in the metal plate that will match the screw you will be using to attach the item.

Attaching Items with Dowel Pins

Using glue and dowel pins is another good way to attach an item, such as the birdhouse on the patriotic whimsy stick shown at the end of the tutorial.

1. Select a wooden dowel pin that suits the size and weight of your item. In this case, a $^3/_8$" pin is used. Drill a $^3/_8$" hole half the length of the dowel pin in the center of your baluster. Add a generous amount of carpenter's wood glue to the hole. Use a foam brush to spread glue onto the pin's surface and push it into the crevices.

2. Spread glue onto the surface of the baluster surrounding the pin.

3. Drill a ³/₈" hole in your item. Place the item onto the pin, being sure to face it in the preferred direction. Push the two parts together. Wipe up any excess glue that may have squirted out onto the baluster. Allow it to dry overnight in an upright position.

Patriotic Whimsy

Decorative birdhouses make great whimsy stick toppers. Note that the entrance hole is blocked with a plastic peace sign that was part of a dollar store necklace. Decorative houses are not suited for bird nesting because they are not weatherproof, not ventilated, and not the precise dimensions birds require. In addition, whimsy sticks are usually placed in the sun, where it will become too hot, and they expose birds to predators because the sticks are so low to the ground.

The house used on this stick was painted with acrylics and sealed with clear acrylic spray. The stick was painted with outdoor enamel. A ¹/₃₂" hole was drilled in the house to accommodate a paper flag of the sort used to decorate cakes. (Many flags come in a package, so you will have plenty of replacements.) The house was attached using the dowel method. Diagonal holes were drilled at angles to match the size of the American flag sticks. The flags are not glued into the holes so they may be removed for storage.

Silver Bird Bath Whimsy

A classier approach was taken with this whimsy. The birdbath top is a collectible hammered aluminum tray, often found at yard sales and antique malls. Magnets were used to affix the removable tray to the stick, making for easy cleaning and storage. The stick is a decorative indoor baluster which was sprayed with regular metallic spray paint. One-inch round mirrors were glued on using waterproof white glue.

Lighthouse Whimsy

This lantern whimsy is attractive by day, useful at night. Pick up a lantern at a yard sale, craft store or where outdoor garden items are sold. Bargains abound right after the major summer holidays. The lantern is attached with magnets so it may be removed to insert a candle or battery-operated tea light. The stick was painted with outdoor enamel, and narrow silver duct tape was wrapped around the stick on the diagonal.

Gazing Ball
for gardeners

Orbs have been a prominent decorative element for centuries. Reflective gazing balls were placed around the home and garden, not for the birds as you might suspect, but to enable people to see others without directly looking their way. Crafty gardeners have found a way to keep thousands of bowling balls from rolling into landfills by decorating them with tiles, glass gems, rocks, broken china, coins, and paint. Recyclers will love this project, as it uses broken clay pots to transform a bowling ball into a beautiful orb that is sure to attract many gazes.

EQUIPMENT

Hammer
Tack hammer
Caulking gun
Tile nippers
Safety glasses
Mixing container for grout
Large bowl or bucket
Measuring cup
Mixing spoon
Old towel
Tarp

SUPPLIES

Broken clay pots
Construction adhesive (Liquid Nails was used for this project.)
Tile grout
Acrylic paint (Red, yellow, sky blue, green, black, and white were used for this project.)
Artist's paintbrush
Latex gloves
Cellulose sponge
Rags or paper towels
Clear acrylic spray
Craft sticks

Light gray or brown grout often does not enhance the design of the ball. Make your orb pop by coloring the grout to match or contrast with the design. Use special grout colorant, available at craft stores, or acrylic artist's paint to do the job.

Used balls sell for a few dollars at yard sales and are often free for the taking at bowling alleys.

This project puts broken clay pot pieces to good use.

Marble or ceramic tiles, glass gems, and river rocks can all be used to transform a bowling ball into a beautiful garden orb.

1. Wipe the ball with mild soapy water to remove dirt and oil. Use a caulking gun to fill the finger holes to the top with construction adhesive. Use a craft stick to smooth the adhesive so that it is flush with the surface of the ball. Wipe off the excess with a wet paper towel.

2. Size the clay pot pieces by thickness. Clay pieces can be any thickness, but they all must be about the same thickness. Place a section of the pot on a piece of plywood, concrete walk, or other hard surface. Place a towel or length of canvas drop cloth over the pot piece. Wear your protective safety glasses while you whack the pot with a hammer. For this project design you need plenty of triangles that measure about 1^1/$_2$" on a side and about a dozen pieces that are ^{1}/$_2$". Other odd shapes will be used to fill in between the design. Continue to break down large pot pieces into usable sizes and shapes.

3. Lay out clay pieces to form the sunflower on your work table or on an old cookie sheet, tray, or plywood board. Create the sunflower by selecting same-sized triangular clay shards for the petals, small triangles and squares for the flower center, and long rectangles for the stem. Leaf shapes may need to be trimmed with the tile nippers. It is helpful to use a pencil to mark the pieces where the flower meets the stem. From petal tip to petal tip, the flower measures 6^1/$_2$". The flower center is about 4" across. Stem pieces are about 1^1/$_2$" long and ^{3}/$_8$" wide and leaves are about 1^1/$_2$" long and ^{1}/$_2$" wide.

4. Use tile nippers to shape the leaves and trim off excess from other pieces. Always wear safety glasses when using nippers. Place the blades where you want the cut to be, and squeeze the handles. For edges, nip off small bits at a time for best results.

5. With the caulking gun, apply adhesive to an area large enough to accommodate the sunflower shape, and use a craft stick to spread the adhesive to the same thickness over the entire area. As you proceed with the design, only apply adhesive to areas you can complete in one sitting.

6. Pull the petals from the design and transfer them to the ball, leaving a consistent ^{3}/$_{16}$" gap between each piece. As you work, slide clay pieces around so that they fall into proper position and even spacing. Fill in the flower center with clay pieces that vary in size and shape.

7. Finding the right shapes to fit the ball can be time consuming. You may have to break additional clay pot sections to get just the right-sized piece. At this point, it is a good idea to start gluing individual pieces. Do this by squirting some adhesive on a scrap ceramic tile or paper plate and using a craft stick to spread a heavy coat on each clay piece.

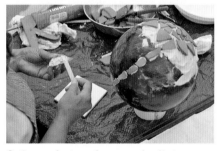

8. Start placing the stem by lining up the marked stem piece with the marked flower petal. Place the stem pieces on the ball, followed by the leaves.

9. If you want to stop at this point and continue later, either scrape off the excess glue or fill in the area with background pieces.

10. As you work, you may find that a clay piece is too thin and drops below the level of the other pieces. You can either find another piece that fits or pull the piece out of the glue with tweezers and add more glue to raise it to the proper level. Replace pieces that are too high, as well. You may be able to nip off the bottom and reuse the piece. Otherwise, find a replacement.

11. Clay pieces that rock back and forth on the ball are too long and must be resized. Reduce the length of a piece so that its entire surface sits flat on the ball.

12. To jazz up the rest of the ball, add three or four smaller flowers consisting of four petal-shaped pieces and one center piece. Glue each piece individually with a craft stick.

13. After all flowers are in place, complete the ball with similarly sized filler pieces. Paint the ball with acrylic colors of your choice. For this project, black was used for the center "seeds."

14. Yellow petals and green stem and leaves complete the sunflower.

15. The smaller flowers were painted red, yellow, and orange, with black or yellow centers and green leaves.

16. White clouds float around the ball against a blue background. Acrylic paints dry quickly, so you can apply a second coat to strengthen the colors soon after the first. Allow the paint to dry for at least twenty-four hours before proceeding.

17. Spray the entire ball with a coat of polyurethane sealant to protect it while grouting.

18. Grout particles are very fine, so you should wear a dust mask and safety glasses while mixing it. (Pre-mixed grout is sold in craft stores, but it is a bit pricey.) Protect your work surface with a tarp or towel. The amount of water to add to grout is determined by feel. Add enough so that the grout will hold together when squeezed—about the consistency of thick peanut butter is a common analogy. It should not fall easily from your spoon. When coloring grout, be sure to make enough for the entire project, as matching the color in a second batch would be difficult. One cup of grout should provide enough for the bowling ball. Fill a measuring cup with $1/4$ cup water and add $1/4$ cup of tube acrylic paint (stop adding paint when the level reaches $1/2$ cup). Slowly pour the water/paint mixture into a larger container filled with a cup of grout. Stir the mixture until it is thoroughly blended, adding water or grout until you reach the correct consistency. Allow the grout to sit for ten minutes, and then remix it lightly.

19. Wear gloves to apply grout. Pick up a handful of grout and spread it across the clay pieces, gently pressing it into the crevices. The grout should be level with the top of the clay pieces.

20. Rotate the ball as needed to cover the entire surface. It is okay if grouted sections sit on your work surface. Allow the grout to set for about fifteen minutes.

21. Wipe off excess grout with a damp sponge. Rinse the grout from the sponge frequently in your water bowl or bucket. Grout will clog sink pipes, so do not let rinse water go down a household drain. Wipe off grout until you see the surface paint show through.

22. A hazy film will remain on the ball. Let the ball rest for about fifteen minutes. Meanwhile, rinse the sponge in the rinse bowl or bucket and dispose of the water outside. Wipe off the haze with a damp rag or paper towel. Set the ball on a towel in the shade to cure for three or four days. Spray on a final coat of polyurethane to offer another layer of protection.

23. Find a prominent place to display your sunflower orb on a pedestal, on a rock, or on the ground. While the orb is weather resistant, it should not be exposed to freezing temperatures.

Applying Square Tiles to a Ball

If you want an orb that has a formal look, place your tiles (or other materials) in straight lines using even spacing. Take time when placing the first row of tiles to ensure it is straight, and use a grout color that complements the tiles.

1. Find the center of the ball by wrapping a tape measure around the middle of the ball to find the circumference. Divide this number in half. In this case, half of the 27" circumference is $13^{1}/_{2}$". Stretch an extra-large rubber band around the middle of the ball. Center it by measuring $13^{1}/_{2}$" from one side to the other side of the band.

2. Squirt some silicone adhesive on a leftover 4" ceramic tile or a paper plate. Use a craft stick to apply the glue to a tile. Place the tile on the ball with one edge touching the rubber band. Continue adding tiles in the same manner, leaving a $^{3}/_{8}$" gap between each tile. After placing four or five tiles, start a second row. Center the tile between the spaces of the tiles below so that the seams don't line up. When you reach the last complete row or two at each of the poles, adjust the tile spacing to fit the last several tiles.

3. If you have time for a long work session, it is much faster to apply adhesive in large sections of the ball. Use a caulking gun to apply adhesive to the ball and use a craft stick to spread it out evenly.

Applying Gems to a Ball

Glass gems really shine in the sun. You don't have to paint your ball if you are happy with the color, but keep in mind that the base color will affect the color of the gems to a slight degree, and that you will see the ball color between the joints of the gems. This ball was painted with white paint for plastics to ensure maximum reflectivity.

1. This a great after-work relaxation project. Hundreds of gems are needed to cover a ball and it takes some time. If you use a tube of clear silicone tile and tub adhesive with a replaceable cap, you can work for any length of time. Apply a generous amount of adhesive to the bottom of the gem and place it anywhere on the ball. Continue adding gems, butting them together as you go.

2. If you are using multiple colors, watch that you are not bunching any one color together. Continue gluing gems until the entire ball is covered. Complete the last 4 square inches or so in one sitting. If that last gem won't fit, slide the rest around while the glue is still wet to fill the empty space. The gem ball is waterproof, but must not be exposed to freezing temperatures.

Balls made with gems look equally good perched on a stump as a focal point, or low to the ground complementing nearby plants.

This ball was adorned with $3/4$" white marble tiles. After the adhesive dried, the tiles were coated with stone and marble tile sealant to prevent the grout colorant from staining the porous tiles. (Sealant does not have to be applied to glazed ceramic tiles.) The ball was grouted with gray grout that was colored with blue acrylic paint, and then was sealed with a coat of polyurethane spray.

Hexagonal
stepping stone

Well-placed paths are a hallmark of good garden design. Make yours stand out with custom-crafted stepping stones. This one uses a two-step process that produces a two-toned stone. If you are intimidated by working with concrete, let this step-by-step project point you in the right direction.

EQUIPMENT

Concrete mixing tub
Old hoe, rake or similar long-handled tool
Garden hand trowel
Flat masonry trowel
2-gallon bucket
Empty gallon jug or water pail
32-ounce measuring cup
Plywood board measuring 2' by 2'
Safety glasses
Dust mask

SUPPLIES

Heavy latex gloves
16" hexagonal stepping stone mold
Bag of premixed, extra-strength concrete
1 cup of mortar
Cooking oil
Liquid concrete strengthener (optional)
Bottle of concrete colorant (terra cotta was used for this project)
2 ounces acrylic paint (dark blue was used for this project)
4" wood letters – N, S, E, W
1" wood bead or ball
Wood piece 1/4" x 2" (square dowel works well)
Duct tape
Craft sticks
Old washcloth or dish towel
Tarp or plastic to protect work surface
Plastic drop cloth to cover mold

About Concrete Mix

Premixed concrete is a combination of cement (made up of lime and clay), stone or gravel, and sand. Water is added to the concrete mix until the proper consistency is reached. Concrete mix and water are measured in parts, not in specific ounces. To assist beginners, this project specifies the quantity of mix and water to begin with. It's a good starting point, but you will need to make adjustments to produce a mix that's not too dry and not too wet.

Ideally, your work area should be shaded so that the concrete doesn't set up too quickly. Covering the stepping stone with plastic also helps to slow down the drying process. You will need a level surface for your mold. A level patch of ground, a picnic table, or a plywood board placed on two saw horses would work well. Molds placed on a plywood board can be moved and leveled if necessary. You will also need a hose to rinse off your tools, but that need not be next to your work space. You can transport the gear to the water. If the weight of the concrete is an issue, enlist help to place the bag in a wheelbarrow or wagon for easy transport.

The extra-strength concrete mix should produce a sufficiently sturdy stepping stone without the addition of concrete fortifier. However, adding it can't hurt and will help to protect it from cracking for many years to come. Adding nylon fibers to the mix is another way to strengthen concrete pieces.

Some important things to remember when working with concrete:

- Always use safety glasses, gloves, and a dust mask when working with the dry material. Concrete and mortar dust are caustic and can burn eyes, lungs, and skin.
- Never rinse tools, bucket, or the mixing tub in a household sink or tub. Use a hose to remove the concrete before it has a chance to dry, and wipe with a towel or rag.
- Store leftover concrete in an airtight storage bin or wrapped in plastic in a dry place.
- Add a little water at a time to the concrete mix; keep blending and adding water until the proper consistency is reached. It's a good idea to have some extra concrete mix on hand should you add too much water. Plan to make more concrete than you need for your project. If you have additional smaller molds on hand, you won't waste any excess concrete. Just don't forget to apply the vegetable oil to help the finished product release easily.

1. Make handles for removing the letters from the concrete. Cut about a 4" length of duct tape. Cut the strip in half.

2. Pinch the sticky sides together, except for $1/4$" on each end.

3. Secure the tape to opposite sides of each letter.

4. By slicing the bag open on the side, you can transport it in a wheelbarrow or wagon. It also can be taped back up for storage.

5. Place the mold on the plywood square. Pour about $1/4$ cup of cooking oil in the mold. This will serve as a release agent for easy removal of the mold from the hardened concrete. Use a paper towel to spread the oil on the bottom and sides of the mold.

6. While wearing your safety gear, use a garden hand trowel to fill the cup, and measure 28 cups of concrete mix into the mixing tub.

7. Fill the measuring cup with 1 cup of water. Pour the desired amount of colorant into the water and stir. Add water to the 32-ounce mark. (The entire 10-ounce bottle of colorant was used in this project to achieve the most intense color possible. This is more than the manufacturer recommends.)

8. Pour the water/colorant solution into the dry concrete mix.

9. Fill the measuring cup with 3 cups of water OR 1 cup of concrete fortifier and 2 cups of water. (Note that concrete fortifier is concentrated and must be diluted per manufacturer's instructions prior to use.)

10. Add the water to the mixing tub and use the long handled tool to blend. As you are mixing, be sure to pull the dry mix from the bottom and incorporate it.

11. At this point, mixing concrete becomes an art. The final mix should not be so dry that it would fall apart if you squeezed and released it, nor should it be runny. Add more water a little at a time. (The water is red because the cup which contained the colorant is being used.)

12. Use the garden hand trowel to shovel concrete into the form.

13. Press out air spaces and push the concrete to the sides of the mold. Pick up one side of the mold and tap it several times on the plywood to distribute the concrete and release any trapped air. Repeat on the other side.

14. Add more concrete if necessary so that it is level with the rim. Switch from the garden trowel to the masonry trowel to smooth the surface of the concrete. If the concrete slides to one side, the mold is not level. Level it up by placing thin boards or sticks under the mold. Tap the mold again and continue smoothing the surface until you are satisfied with the appearance.

15. Press the letters into the concrete until they are level with the surface, positioning them by eye so that they are about the same distance away from the edge. Place the 1" bead or ball halfway into the concrete in the center of the mold.

16. Grasp the tape handles and pull the letters straight up to remove them. Carefully remove the bead or ball.

17. Depress the edge of the craft stick between the ball and the letters to make directional lines at the same depth as the letters. At this point, the concrete is still workable. If you are not happy with your impressions, re-trowel the surface smooth and try again.

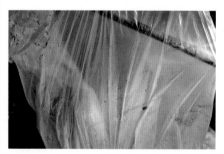

18. Cover the mold with plastic, propping it up so that it doesn't touch the concrete. Use any leftover concrete to make a small stepping stone or other items. Rinse off tools before the concrete dries. Do not allow concrete to run down a household drain.

19. Allow the covered concrete to set up in the shade for two or three days. (Set up time will vary depending on the air temperature and water content of the mix.) Flip the stepping stone over and pull the mold off of the concrete.

20. Don your safety gear and prepare a batch of mortar. Place 1 cup of mortar into a large measuring cup. In a separate cup, mix $1/2$ cup water with $1/4$ cup of dark blue acrylic paint. Add the water/paint solution to the dry powder and stir. Adjust the water/mortar mix as necessary to achieve a paste-type consistency.

21. Use a craft stick to place the mortar into the grooves of the letters, pressing it into the corners with your finger.

22. A wet washcloth or dishcloth works well to remove any unwanted mortar surrounding the letter.

23. Allow your stepping stone to fully cure for thirty days before using it in a prominent spot in the garden.

Concrete
leaf bowl

Made from a *Hosta* leaf, this charming bowl blends with a natural setting. Place several bowls around your garden, both on pedestals and on the ground, to benefit a range of wildlife. A bowl on the patio or deck makes for an attractive pet water bowl. You can make many bowls for the price of just one commercially-made birdbath top, and use the leftover concrete to make decorative plates, as well.

EQUIPMENT

Small bucket

5-gallon bucket

Empty 1-gallon jug or water pail

32-ounce measuring cup

Garden hand trowel

Masonry trowel

Plywood board, about 2' by 2'

**Concrete sanding block or chunk of
   cinder block**

Safety glasses

Dust mask

SUPPLIES

Large plant leaf* (*Hosta* **Sum and
   Substance was used for this
   project.)**

Bag Portland cement

Bag all-purpose sand

Acrylic paint

Artist's paintbrush

**Tarp or heavy sheet plastic to fit
   plywood board**

**Plastic drop cloth or similar to cover
   project**

Heavy latex gloves

Concrete fortifier (optional)

**Chicken wire – ¹/₂" or 1" mesh
   (optional)**

***If you would like to make use of any
   leftover concrete, cut a smaller leaf
   or two, as well.**

About Portland Cement

Portland cement is a combination of
lime and clay and is named after the
British island where it was formulated. Once it is mixed with aggre-
gates (such as sand, gravel, rocks,
etc.) and water, it becomes concrete.
This particular concrete recipe uses
sand and water, but no stone.

Ideally, your work area should be
shaded so that the concrete doesn't
set up too quickly. Covering the
cement with plastic also helps to slow
down the drying process. Make your
bowl on a plywood board covered
with heavy plastic or a tarp. You will
also need a hose to rinse off your
tools, but that need not be next to
your work space. You can transport
the gear to the water. If the weight of
the cement and sand is an issue,
enlist help to place the bags in a
wheelbarrow or wagon for easy transport.

This project illustrates how to add
concrete fortifier and chicken wire to
increase the strength of the bowl. The
concrete mix alone will produce a rea-
sonably strong bowl, so you can make
your bowl without using either item.
However, if you have them on hand,
adding one or both will help protect
the bowl from cracking for many
years to come. Nylon fibers are also
sold as another option to strengthen
concrete pieces.

Some important things to remember when working with cement:

- Always use safety glasses, gloves,
  and a dust mask when working
  with the dry material. Portland
  cement dust is caustic and can burn
  eyes, lungs, and skin.
- Never rinse tools, bucket, or the
  mixing tub in a household sink or
  tub. Use a hose to remove Portland
  cement or concrete before it has a
  chance to dry, and wipe with a
  towel or rag.
- Store leftover Portland cement in
  an airtight storage bin or wrapped
  in plastic in a dry place.
- Add a little water at a time to the
  Portland cement mix. Keep blending and adding water until the
  proper consistency is reached. It's a
  good idea to have some extra Portland cement on hand should you
  add too much water. Plan to make
  more concrete than you need for
  your project. Have additional
  smaller molds on hand to use up
  excess concrete.

1. Prepare your work space by placing
the plywood on a sturdy surface and
covering it with heavy sheet plastic
that is cut to fit. Before opening the
bag of Portland cement, put on
gloves, dust mask, and safety glasses
as protection from the dust. If you
slice the cement bag on its side, the
bag can be easily taped to store leftover material. Cut a large *Hosta* or
other plant leaf from the garden.

2. Fill a small bucket with sand using
the garden hand trowel. Add a little
water to moisten it just so it sticks
together when squeezed. It should
not be runny.

3. Make a sand mound on the plywood that is the approximate size of your leaf.

4. Pack down the sand mound and shape it so that the center is several inches higher than the sizes. The surface of the sand mound will become the depression in the bowl.

5. Place the leaf on the sand mound and adjust the shape of the mound to fit. Remove excess sand so that the sloped edges of the leaves touch the board.

6. Cut the stem off close to the leaf and replace the leaf on the mound. Use the masonry trowel to remove excess sand. The edges of the leaf should touch the board. Reduce the height of the mound if necessary.

7. Quantities of ingredients to make concrete are measured in parts. This recipe calls for 1 part cement to 3 parts sand. Water is added last until the correct consistency is reached. Here, a large coffee can is used to place two full containers of Portland cement and six full containers of sand into a 5-gallon bucket. Use the trowel to blend the cement and sand as you add them.

8. The addition of concrete fortifier is not essential, but will add strength to

Patching Holes in Leaves

Should your leaf have a hole in it, simply cut a square from another similarly-sized leaf and place the square over the hole, matching the veins.

your project. Measure 1 cup of fortifier and 3 cups of water (or 4 cups plain water), and pour this slowly into the bucket containing the Portland cement/sand mixture.

9. Use the garden hand trowel to blend the ingredients until they are completely incorporated. Add water a little at a time and continue to blend until your mixture is thoroughly moistened. The final mix should hold together when squeezed, but should not be runny.

11. Another way to strengthen your concrete bowl is to place chicken wire between two layers of the cement. (You can use fortifier and/or chicken wire in the same project, but both are optional.) Cut the wire to fit the center of the bowl. It should not extend over the edges.

14. Use the trowel to smooth the entire surface. Flatten the rounded center of the mound by pressing down with the trowel. Estimate the size of the base that will be needed to keep the bottom of the bowl from rocking. Eye it up from all sides to ensure that it is level.

10. Use your gloved hand to scoop out some concrete and place it over the leaf. Continue until you have about a $3/4$" layer over the entire leaf. (Note that if you are not going to add chicken wire to your bowl, as shown in steps 11 through 13, increase the thickness of this layer to about $1^1/2$".) Press the material down and together as you go. Be sure to cover the stem end with plenty of concrete. One technique to ensure a consistent layer of material is to form same-sized concrete patties and place them adjacent to one another.

12. Add another $1/2$" to $3/4$" of cement to cover the chicken wire completely. Press it down and pack it together as you go.

15. Cover the concrete bowl with plastic and allow to cure for two or three days.

13. Cut off excess concrete from the edges of the bowl using the masonry trowel. Use your gloved hand to smooth the concrete edges which touch the board.

16. Use the plastic sheeting if necessary to help you grasp the edge of the bowl to flip it over.

17. Most of the *Hosta* leaf will peel off, revealing a beautiful replica of the leaf veining.

18. Use a whisk broom to remove any leaf bits that remain.

19. You may be satisfied with any rough edges on the rim. If not, you can sand them down using a concrete sanding block or a chunk of cinder block.

20. Let the bowl cure completely for thirty days before painting it. Use the whisk broom to brush off any loose material on the top and bottom of the bowl.

21. There are a lot of options for finishing your bowl. You can use one color all over. Here, light green acrylic paint was used for the top and dark green was used for the bottom. You can mimic two-toned leaves by painting the center one color and the edges a second color. You may even choose to go in a different direction altogether and paint your bowl a wild blue, purple, orange, or whatever pleases you.

22. Once the bowl is dry, you can accentuate the leaf veining. Mix a dark green acrylic paint with a little water to thin it. Work quickly to paint the center vein and the side veins on one half of the bowl.

23. Use a damp paper towel or rag to wipe the paint from the surface of the bowl before it has a chance to dry. Don't wipe off the paint that has settled into the veins. Repeat the process on the other side.

24. Allow the bowl to cure for several weeks in a warm, dry area. Your *Hosta* leaf bowl is ready to be filled and placed in the garden.

This is an alternate leaf project you could try.

Enhance
the deck & patio

Watermelon Slice
punk holder

Punk is an old-fashioned incense stick whose smoke is used to shoo away mosquitoes, gnats and other pesky insects. The aroma of punk is unusual, unmistakable, and quite pleasant to most. It's a better alternative to chemical-laden insect sprays and lotions. Punk is still available at hardware stores and online. When those buggy summer days arrive, you will want to give this folk art watermelon slice a prominent spot on the deck or patio and fire up the punk.

EQUIPMENT

Chainsaw or 24" or 36" bow saw
Wood vise
Palm sander with medium grit paper
¹/₂" wood chisel
Hammer
Drill with ¹/₈" bit
Artist's paintbrushes
1" or 2" foam or chip brush

SUPPLIES

Wood primer paint
Paper or foam plate
**Acrylic paint—black, white, green,
  red, yellow**
Punk sticks
Hardwood wedge
Clear acrylic spray

Selecting Wood

Choose a dried hardwood log that is at least 10" in diameter. If you use a freshly cut log, you must allow the individual wedges to dry prior to sanding and painting them, or they may crack as the wood dries.

1. Estimate the width of the slice, or make two marks on the log about 5" apart. Saw one side of the slice at an angle to the center of the log. Saw the other side at the same angle, again stopping at the center of the log where it meets the first cut. Continue sawing slices until you reach the end of the log. Then, flip the log over and cut more wedges between the ones you just cut.

2. Place the chisel between the wood and the bark and tap lightly on the chisel until the bark pops off.

3. Use a palm sander or hand sanding block and medium grit sandpaper to smooth the sides and the bottom. This is a rustic piece, so the goal is to sand off splinters and rough edges, not to make the wedge tabletop smooth.

4. If your wedge was cut to the exact center, you should see a tree ring that's perfect for the bite hole.

5. Tap gently on the chisel as you move it along the tree ring line. The piece should release easily.

6. A rotary tool or a piece of medium grit sandpaper can be used to clean up any splintered wood on the depression and the long edge. If your wedge does not have a small tree ring at the edge, use a handheld rotary tool with a sanding disk to create your own. This may be made at the center or off to one side.

7. Paint the piece with a generous coat of wood primer and allow it to dry.

8. Use a pencil to mark locations for four holes on each side. Place them about 2" from the bottom edge and about 2" apart.

9. Use a $5/32$" drill bit to make the holes. (Check to ensure your punk sticks will fit and adjust if necessary.) To keep the bit from slipping on the slanted piece, start drilling with your bit at a right angle to the piece, then quickly move it so that is at about a 45-degree angle. Drill as deep as the bit will allow.

10. Make puddles of white, red, and yellow paint on your palette. Use a flat artist's brush to paint about a $3/8$" border around the bottom edge of the wedge to resemble the watermelon rind and allow it to dry. Paint the fruit of the watermelon a straight bright red, or mix in a little white to make a pink tint.

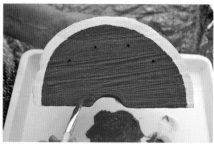

11. Another interesting color can be made by adding a bit of yellow to make a salmon-pink. Experiment with color mixing to get the color you like. Make enough of the mix to cover the whole wedge, since color matching can be difficult. Load up your brush with plenty of paint, and paint the curve where the rind meets the fruit. Don't worry if you goof a bit on this step; a touch up is often needed on the rind after the bottom is painted. Paint the body of the wedge, being sure to push paint into the wood indentations. Paint the edge. Paint the other side in the same manner and allow the wedge to dry.

12. Place puddles of green and black paint on your palette. Darken the green with a touch of black. Starting at one of the points, paint the outside edges of the watermelon skin stripes in a wavy pattern. Paint the center stripes, making them thin at the points and thicker in the center. Add light green to the paint palette. While the dark green is still wet, paint the in-between stripes with the same wavy pattern. Allow this coat to dry.

13. Apply a second coat of both colors to the bottom. After this coat dries, touch up the white rind if necessary.

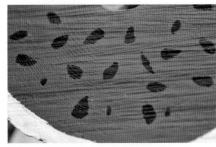

14. Use an artist's brush to paint the seeds. A round brush with a sharp point or the narrow side of a flat brush work well. Use black paint to apply a teardrop shape. Your watermelon slice will be more interesting if you paint seeds in varying widths, at irregular intervals, and differing orientations.

15. Use white to paint thin highlight stripes along one edge.

16. Highlights are painted on the same sides of objects to show the direction of the light, but it isn't a must in this instance.

17. Extend the life of your punk holder by spraying it with a coat of clear acrylic, polyurethane, or spar varnish.

Cork Plant Stand
or side table

This table takes the cork-lined coaster to a new level. The cork top will absorb moisture from plant pots and drinking glasses alike. The dark chunky cork meshes well with the lighter, fine-grained cork trim. Fabric or wallpaper can be easily tacked to the support post for endless design possibilities. Cork products are in plentiful supply and usually on sale during the months preceding the start of school. The table will provide years of use as an indoor plant stand or side table on a covered deck or patio.

EQUIPMENT

Drill with $^3/_{16}$" bit
Wood vise
Hacksaw
Caulking gun
3" or 4" putty knife
Straight edge
Flexible seamstress
   measuring tape
T-square
Craft knife
Self-healing mat or
   other cutting
   surface
Pencil

SUPPLIES

Light brown cork roll, 2' x 4'
12" x 12" dark brown cork squares (4)
Plywood square, $^1/_2$" x 12" x 12"
High-density hardboard (HDF)
   panel*, $^3/_8$" x 12" x 12"
2" x 2$^1/_4$" pine wood blocks (2)
Scrap 2" x 4" board (a 1' long board is
   sufficient)
23" segment of 3" PVC pipe (outside
   diameter is 3$^1/_2$")
Tube construction adhesive
1$^5/_8$" galvanized deck screws (6)
Clear, waterproof, permanent
   bonding adhesive (E-6000 was
   used in this project)
Thumbtacks or push pins
12" x 12" paper for pattern
*HDF is sometimes referred to as
   "Masonite," which is a defunct
   brand name. Many hardware and
   lumber stores will offer to cut the
   large panels down to a
   manageable size at no charge.
   Hardboard is also available in
   small sizes at art supply stores.

3. Measure and mark a point $^3/_4$" from the top of the pipe, and roughly in the center of the block. With the pipe secured in a vise, screw a 1$^5/_8$" galvanized deck screw at the mark, through the PVC pipe and into the 2" side of the wood block. Flip the pipe over and secure the pipe to the wood block on this side. Repeat the process at the other end of the pipe.

1. With the hacksaw, cut a 23" length of the PVC pipe. Use a hammer to pound the 2" x 2$^1/_4$" block partway into the pipe opening.

2. Place a scrap piece of 2" x 4" pine board over the block and pound it until it is flush with the top of the PVC pipe. Repeat at the other end of the pipe.

4. Make an "X" in the wood block and mark the center. Drill a pilot hole using $^1/_{16}$" drill bit.

5. Find and mark the center of the 12" x 12" hardboard panel. Drill a deck screw partway into the center of the panel, leaving about $1/2$" exposed. Apply some construction adhesive on the block. Line up the screw and the pilot hole, and finish screwing the hardboard to the wood block.

7. Center one of the 12" x 12" dark cork squares on the hardboard. Press it in place, making sure that the entire surface area is pressed into the adhesive.

10. Center the paper on one of the 12" x 12" dark brown cork squares. Use thumbtacks or push pins to attach the paper to the cork square at the corners and on either side of the circle.

6. Apply construction adhesive on the edges and the center of the hardboard panel. Use a putty knife to smooth out the adhesive in an even layer up to all edges.

8. Make an "X" on the 12" x 12" paper pattern by drawing lines from corner to corner. Make a pencil mark in the center where the lines meet. Center a small segment of PVC pipe on the paper using the center mark as a guide. Do a quick check by measuring from the edge to the pipe on two adjacent sides.

11. With the pattern as a guide, cut out a disk from the cork, using a sawing motion with the craft knife.

9. Trace the outline of the centered pipe. Place the paper on a self-healing mat or other cutting surface, and use a craft knife to cut out the circle.

12. Clean up the edges of the circle.

13. Check to see that the hole is properly cut by gently pushing the cork square onto the PVC pipe. If it resists, locate the trouble spot, remove the cork square, and widen the hole slightly at that point. Repeat the process to cut a hole in a second cork square.

14. With the pipe facing up, gently push the 12" x 12" dark cork square halfway down the PVC pipe.

15. Apply a generous amount of construction adhesive to the hardboard and use the putty knife to smooth it evenly on the board, around the PVC pipe.

16. Push the cork square down until it meets the hardboard, and press it evenly into the construction adhesive.

17. Determine the length of cork sheet needed to wrap around the PVC pipe by measuring the circumference of the pipe and adding $1^{1}/_{4}$" to compensate for the thickness of the cork. In this instance, it is $11^{1}/_{8}$" plus $1^{1}/_{4}$", to equal $12^{3}/_{8}$".

18. Unroll the cork, place it on a self-healing mat or other cutting surface, and use the T-square to flatten it out. Place the T-square at the $12^{3}/_{8}$" mark and use a utility knife to cut the cork. Trim the long side from 24" to $23^{1}/_{4}$" with the T-square and utility knife.

19. Work fast to apply two lines of permanent bonding adhesive near all edges of the cork. (Do NOT follow product instructions that may advise applying glue to both surfaces and

waiting until the glue cures before bringing the surfaces together. The glue will form an immediate bond and you will not be able to reposition the cork if it is misaligned.) As soon as you finish applying the glue, put the cork in place around the PVC pipe and match the seams.

20. Use wide masking tape to hold the cork together while the glue cures. Tape each end and the center first and then fill in the gaps with tape. Make sure the center seam is together along the entire length and that the wrapped cork is flush with the dark cork base. Allow the glue to cure overnight, and then remove the tape.

21. Find and mark the center of the ¹/₂" x 12" x 12" plywood square.

22. Flip the board over; use the caulking gun to apply construction adhesive and a putty knife to smooth out the adhesive over the entire board. (Note: This board had been primed for another project. Priming is not necessary.)

23. Center the cork square with the hole over the plywood board and press it down, making sure that the entire surface is adhered to the board.

24. Align the hold in the bottom to the PVC pipe.

25. Screw a 1⁵/₈" deck screw through the center of the board and into the wood block.

26. Apply construction adhesive to the board, and even it out with a putty knife. Center the fourth dark brown cork square to the board, and press it into place.

27. Lay the table on its side, and align the top and the bottom. Let the adhesive dry and cure for twenty-four hours.

28. Accurately measure the widths of the top and the bottom panels of the table. In this instance, they are 1" and 1³/₈", respectively.

29. Measure, mark, and cut four strips of cork sheet in your top width measurement and four strips in your bottom width measurement.

30. Measure and cut the bottom edge strips to fit the two opposite sides of the table base panel. Apply permanent bonding adhesive along the length of the strip, and use a small piece of cork to spread out the adhesive to the edges in an even layer. Attach the strips to the panel right away, aligning all edges.

31. Tape the strips to the panel to hold them in place while the adhesive cures. Repeat the process for the table top.

32. When you measure the edge strips for the remaining two sides, measure from the outer edges of the cork strips that are in place. Cut the remaining strips, and glue and tape them in place. Allow the glue to cure overnight.

33. If you wish to dress up the cork seam, cut a 1" strip of cork to fit the post length. Place thumbtacks several inches apart along the post to secure the strip.

34. Fabric or wallpaper can be used to add a colorful design to your post. Fasten the material with thumbtacks so that it is easily replaceable.

35. Your lightweight but sturdy cork table is ready to be used as a side table or plant stand.

Macramé
plant hanger

During the heyday of modern macramé in the 1970s, enthusiastic knot tiers turned out everything from fashion accessories (belts, necklaces, headbands and handbags) to large home décor (wall panels and hanging tables and chairs). As a result of the resurgence of houseplant tending, the one macramé item found in almost every home was the hanging plant holder. By learning to tie two knots, you can ditch the ugly metal or plastic hanger for one that will enhance your potted plant. And you'll enjoy a groovy crafting experience while doing so.

EQUIPMENT

Scissors

SUPPLIES

50 yards macramé cord

3 yards blue paracord (Paracord is a nylon cord sold in craft stores. This is only needed if you want colored bands at the hanging loop and base.)

1" colored wood beads (3)

¹/₂" colored wood beads (12)

12 heavy duty rubber bands

Hanging basket container

About Cord

The most common cords used for macramé hangers are made of jute, nylon and cotton. Nylon clothesline is used for this tutorial as it is easy to work with and inexpensive. To estimate the length of cord you will need, take the length of the hanger you want to make, multiply by four, and then double. That number is the length of each cord you will cut.

How many cords do you need? For a hanger that has three knotted arms, you need six cords. If you want four arms, you would need eight cords.

For example, if you wanted a hanger measuring one yard, multiply one yard by four and you get four yards. Double that number equals eight yards. The cord length is eight yards. There are three arms in the hanger, so you need six cords, each eight yards long. (The amount of cord needed will decrease if the hanger is not heavily knotted.)

Tying the Square Knot

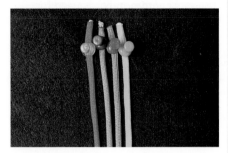

1. The knot-bearing cords are the two inside cords. The working cords are the two outer cords.

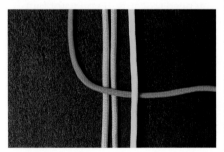

2. To tie a square knot, take the left working cord over the two knot-bearing cords and under the right working cord.

3. Send the right working cord under the left working cord, behind the two knot-bearing cords and over the left working cord.

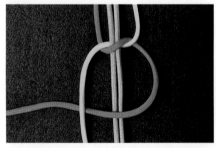

4. You'll see that the left and right working cords have switched places. Take the right working cord over the

two knot-bearing cords and under the left working cord.

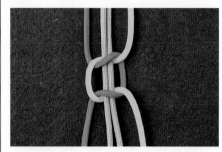

5. Send the left working cord under the right working cord, behind the two knot-bearing cords, through the loop and over the right working cord.

6. Tighten the completed knot. Notice that the right (yellow) working cord forms the vertical bar on the left. Reverse the steps to form a bar on the right.

7. Take the right working cord over the left working cord. Send it over the left working cord, behind the two knot-bearing cords, through the loop and over the left working cord. Another vertical bar has been created.

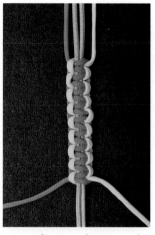

8. A series of square knots such as this is called a sinnet.

Tying the Spiral Knot

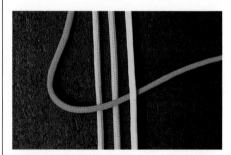

1. Place the left working cord over the knot-bearing cords and under the right working cord.

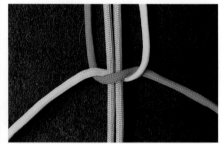

2. Repeat the process. Take the left working cord (which is now the red cord) over the knot-bearing cords and under the right working cord (which is now the yellow cord).

3. This is how your spiral sinnet will look after you've made a few knots. You will notice that the working cords will start spiraling.

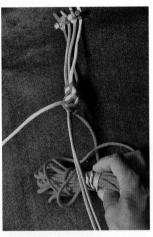

4. At the point where the left working cord is almost straight up and down, you will need to flip the cords. Do so by holding onto the left working cord and sliding the right working cord under the knot-bearing cords. This will flatten out the sinnet so that you can continue knotting.

5. This is how a half knot spiral will look.

Make the Plant Hanger

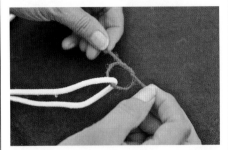

1. Measure and cut six cords that are six yards in length. Find the center of each cord and tie a string at that mark.

2. Keep the ends from fraying by taping with masking or cellophane tape. Nylon cord may be secured by touch-

ing a flame to the end. The cord will melt, not erupt in a flame. It will be hot, so wait about ten seconds before touching it.

3. Butterfly the cords into a bundle. Place one end of the cord over your palm behind your thumb and between your little and ring fingers with the tail facing up. Let the rest of the cord lie on the floor.

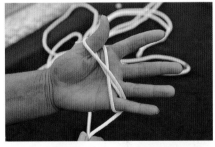

4. Bring the cord up across your palm and around your thumb. Bring the cord down and between your ring and middle fingers. Wrap the cord around your little finger and back up.

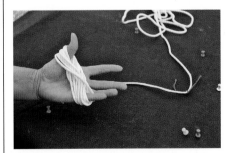

5. Continue to bring the cord up around your thumb and back down between your two fingers. Don't wrap the cord too tight or you won't be able to remove your fingers. Stop wrapping when you are about a foot away from the center mark.

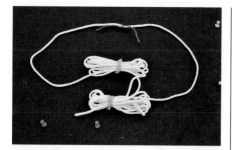

6. Pull the bundle off your hand and wrap a rubber band around it several times. Butterfly the remaining cords.

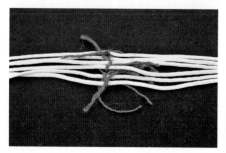

7. Line up the centers of each cord.

8. Use a pencil to make two marks on one of the cords, 2¹/₂" on either side of center.

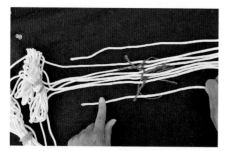

9. Cut two cords 48" long. Line them up on either side of the cords about 2" above one of the marks you just made.

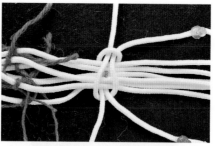

10. Tie a square knot around the six cords on top of the mark. It is the same process as shown in the tutorial except instead of having two knot-bearing cords, you have six.

11. Pull the knot tight. Remove the strings that marked the cord centers.

12. Continue making square knots until you reach the second mark. This sinnet should be about 5" long.

13. This sinnet will serve as the hanging loop. If you would prefer a metal hanging ring, now is the time to add one by threading the six bundles from the same side of the project through the ring and up to the center of the square knot sinnet. Metal rings are beneficial in that they can slide onto almost any size "S" hook or shepherd's hook arm. A ring is especially useful when working with heavy-weight jute cord.

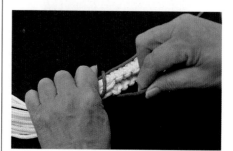

14. Secure the hanging loop. Cut a 36" length of cord. You may use the same project cord as the hanger or another cord in a contrasting color. Here, blue paracord is being used. Fold the square knot sinnet in half. Form a loop near the end of the blue cord with the tail facing upward. Hold the loop in place as you wrap the long end of the blue cord around all twelve cords, starting at the base of the square knot sinnet. Pull the blue cord firmly as you wrap.

15. Wrap about 1½" with the blue cord. On your last wrap, feed the end of the cord through the loop and cut it off, leaving about 2".

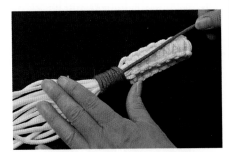

16. Grasp the 2" cord you just cut and pull firmly on the tail end of the cord at the top. This will pull the bottom loop up under the wrap.

17. Cut off the blue cord tail at the top and tuck it into the wrapped cord. Cut all loose ends from the square knot sinnet that made up the hanging loop. Be sure not to cut off any of the long cords that are butterflied.

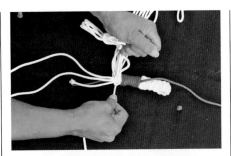

18. Divide your butterflied bundles into three sets of four cords each. Start tying spiral knots with one group of four cords. Pull cord out from each butterfly bundle as you need it. Stop when the sinnet is 5" long and move the tied cord aside. Collect another four cords and tie another 5" sinnet of spiral knots. Do the same with the third bundle. Pick up the cords by the hanging loop and make sure all three sinnets are even.

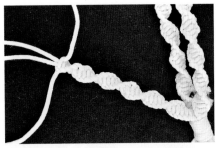

19. Select one of the sinnets and untie the butterfly bundles of the two working cords. Thread the two cords through a 1" bead and push it up to the sinnet.

20. Up to now, you have been using a lot of working cord to make the spiral knot, but not as much of the knot-

bearing cord. Some patterns will instruct you to reverse the cords. This will enable you to use less cord for your projects. To do so, just bring the working cords to the center and use the knot-bearing cords to tie the next knot. At this point, tie a square knot, pushing it close to the bead. Continue tying square knots until you complete a 5" sinnet.

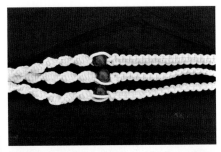

21. Repeat the process with the other two bundles of cord.

22. Begin making the cradle for your pot by measuring the circumference around the top of the pot. Divide this number by twice the number of sinnets in the hanger. This hanger has three sinnets, so we will divide by six. The pot circumference in this case is about 28" divided by six, which is a little over 4½". This provides an estimate of how far apart the cradle cords will extend.

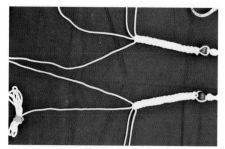

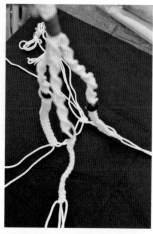

23. Making the cradle is a bit difficult to illustrate. Sometimes, it may appear that there is just a jumble of cords. The goal is to attach all three groups of cords together to form a sling to hold the pot. Start by placing two sinnets toward you and the third out of the way. Separate the cords to go in two opposite directions.

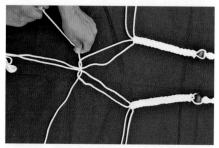

24. Take two cords from one sinnet and two cords from another, and tie a loose square knot about $4^{1}/_{2}$" down from the knotted cord.

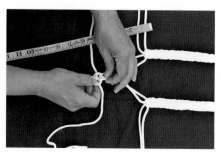

25. The distance between the knotted cord and the square knot should be $4^{1}/_{2}$" on each side. Use a tape measure to confirm the length. Once the sides are even, tighten the square knot.

26. Pick up the hanger by the loop and twist the sinnets around so that this time, you will be connecting the cord bundle you just knotted with the next adjacent cord bundle. (The cords hanging down in Step 26 will be connected to two cords in the next bundle, which has not yet been knotted.)

27. It is helpful to move all cords out of the way except the ones you are working with. Tie another square knot $4^{1}/_{2}$" down from the ends of the square knot sinnets. Pick up the hanger again and twist it around so that you can knot the final group of cords. You should be left with two cords from one tied section and two cords from the other. Tie a square knot using these four cords.

28. Suspend the hanger and insert your pot. This is how your hanger should look. If the knots are a bit off center, adjust them now.

29. Finish the cradle by tying three more square knots. These knots will fall in between the knots you just made right beneath the square knot sinnets. Set the hanger down with the pot still in it and spread out the cords as shown. You should be able to visualize tying the cords that face you to make the bottom portion of the cradle.

30. This pot's sides are fairly straight, so we will use the same 4¹/₂" measurement for the second row of the cradle. (If you make a hanger for a pot with deeply sloped sides, you would measure the circumference lower on the pot and recalculate this number as in Step 22.) This time, measure from the square knots you just made to position the second row of square knots.

31. This is how your hanger should look with the addition of the second row of square knots. Adjust the spacing between all the knots.

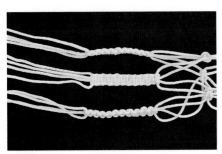

32. Finish the cradle by continuing to make square knots that will go beneath the pot and meet in the center. If you measure the width of the bottom of the pot and divide by two, you will have an approximate length of each square knot sinnet.

33. Secure all twelve cords with a rubber band where they meet the square knot sinnets. Check the fit of the pot again at this point. Remove or add square knots as needed so that the pot fits snugly in the hanger.

34. Use the project cord or blue paracord to cover the rubber band, using the same process you used for the wrap at the top.

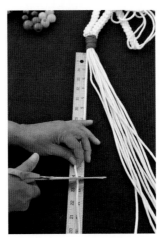

35. Cut all twelve cords about 12" from the bottom wrap.

36. String a ¹/₂" bead onto one cord and tie an overhand knot. To make an overhand knot, make a loop, thread the lose end through it, and tighten.

37. Continue stringing beads at different levels along the cord. Cut the cords close to the beads.

38. To prevent the ends of the nylon cord from fraying, singe them with a lighter or flame from a candle.

Adding Shells to Plant Hangers

Seashells are an attractive alternative to beads on a macramé hanger. The trick to drilling the hanging hole is to use duct tape to secure the shell to a thick piece of merchandise packing foam. Use a drill bit that's appropriate for the size cord you are using. Put light downward pressure on the drill as it spins. The bit will suddenly pop through and go into the foam. Keep the drill running as you carefully pull it out of the shell hole.

If you are using multi-ply cord, unravel a 6" to 8" length. Thread both ends through the shell hole and through the loop. Tie the shell to the knot-bearing cords, cut off the loose ends and continue making knots.

With a handmade macramé hanger, your plants can hang at eye level, where they can be best viewed and watered.

This heavy duty hanger was made with 4-ply, 72# jute twine using the same pattern as the one in the tutorial. A large, wooden doll-head ball was painted red to adorn the bottom of the pot.

Two-Tiered
planter

This three-in-one planter can be used for live or artificial plants, indoors or outdoors. Showcase your cascading and trailing plants in the top basket. Flowering annuals or leafy houseplants are equally at home in the bottom clay pot. The center post can support live or artificial vines. The space-saving design is perfect for balconies or small-space areas and it provides height to a grouping of containers.

EQUIPMENT

Hammer or tack hammer

Drill with $^1/_{16}$" bit and $^1/_8$" bit

Torpedo level

SUPPLIES

10" or 12" wire hanging basket with
    coco liner

14" or 16" clay pot

Deck post

Round wooden disk, about $^1/_2$" thick
    ($5^1/_2$" disk was used in this project)

Outdoor enamel or deck stain

Acrylic paints (green, oxide of
    chromium, phthalo blue,
    ultramarine blue, and burnt umber
    were used in this project)

Mortar mix

Ruler or tape measure

$^1/_4$" wire staples

2 synthetic artist sponges or sea
    sponges

Construction adhesive

48" length of $^1/_4$" flexible tube

$1^5/_8$" galvanized deck screw

2. Pick up some of the light green paint with the edge of a well-wrung artist sponge or sea sponge. Dab it onto the pot randomly, rotating the direction of the sponge each time. Flip the sponge around and dab the clean corner into the darker green paint, dabbing it on alongside the light green. With a second sponge, pick up some phthalo blue and dab it over and between the two greens. When your sponge becomes too dirty to use, rinse and squeeze out as much water as possible.

1. Sponge paint the clay pot, the deck post, and the $5^1/_2$" disk. Use a foam plate or paper plate as a palette for your puddles of paint.

3. Blend the edges of the colors, but do not muddy them by over-sponging the same area. Be sure to paint the under edge of the rim, and about 5" down from the top on the inside of the pot. If you prefer more contrast between the light and dark greens, mix a little burnt umber into the ultramarine blue and use the clean edge of the phthalo blue sponge to apply it.

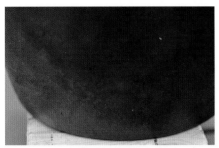

4. Keep working the pot until you are satisfied with the results.

5. Once the paint dries, you can further embellish it by using stamps. This fleur-de-lis was stamped on with metallic gold acrylic paint. Keep in mind that foam stamps will bend to fit the curvature of the pot. Small rubber stamps will work, but larger ones may not yield good results.

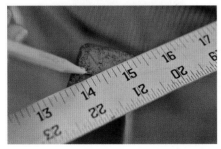

6. Find the center of the deck post by drawing an "X" from corner to corner with a straight edge.

7. Use a $^1/_{16}$" drill bit to make a pilot hole about $^1/_2$" deep at the center mark.

8. To find the center of the disk, trace the outline on a piece of paper and cut it out. Fold the paper in half and in half again. The center is where the two creases meet. Transfer the center point onto the disk with a pencil.

9. Drill a pilot hole at the center mark on the disk using a $^1/_8$" bit. Screw a $1^5/_8$" galvanized deck screw through the disk so that about $^1/_2$" sticks out of the bottom.

10. Apply construction adhesive to the top of the deck post.

11. Tilt the disk so that you can align the screw to the pilot hole. Straighten the disk and fasten the screw into the post.

12. Use a damp paper towel to clean up any adhesive that squirted out.

13. Attaching the wire basket to the disk can be tricky. Place a wire staple across one of the basket wires. Use a hammer (or smaller tack hammer) to pound the staple in. If the basket sides interfere, try placing a hammer head over the staple and hitting it with another hammer.

14. Should that prove to be difficult, drill two pilot holes at the staple points with a very small $^1/_{32}$" bit. Position the staple in the pilot holes and hammer it in.

15. Cut four 12" lengths of $^1/_4$" tubing. Use duct tape to secure the tubes on the center of each side of the post so that about 2" extends beyond the post.

16. Tape together the post and the four tubes close to the bottom of the post.

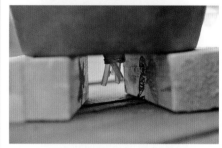

17. Place the pot on two wood blocks to raise it up. Insert the post into the pot so that the tube bundle protrudes from the drainage hole.

18. Cover the drainage hole and secure the tube bundle with duct tape.

19. Use a torpedo level to ensure the pot is level on all sides.

20. Put on your dust mask, safety glasses and gloves to mix a batch of mortar. Measure enough mortar to fill about one-third of the clay pot. Add water and stir until the mortar is thoroughly moistened, but not runny. It should be the consistency of brownie mix.

21. Use your gloved hand or a trowel to fill the clay pot, compressing the mortar as you go to remove any air pockets.

22. Adjust the tubes so that they are about ¼" away from the post.

23. Use a torpedo level to ensure that the post is level on all sides.

24. Place strips of duct tape on all four sides of the post to keep it straight while the mortar dries. Check the post again after taping to be sure it is still level. Allow the mortar to dry.

25. Remove the tape from the bottom of the pot and cut the tubes flush with the pot.

26. Cut the tubes on the inside of the pot flush with the mortar.

27. Fill the pot and the basket with soilless planting mix and add your favorite plants.

Use your two-tiered planter to brighten up a shady area and add height to groundcovers with colorful annuals such as these Dragon Wing Begonias. The lime-leaf Heuchera in the top basket will be moved to a perennial bed at the end of the growing season.

Decoupage
chairs

Chairs are a high-demand and low-supply essential at garden parties. The crafty solution is to spruce up those old chairs that have been sitting in the attic or garage for years or your inexpensive yard sale finds. Start the transformation with fresh paint and new seat fabric. Then apply paper embellishments using the modern decoupage process. You're sure to get a lot of compliments from your party guests.

EQUIPMENT

Staple gun with ¼" staples

Scissors, short- and long-handled

SUPPLIES

Wooden chair (One with a removable covered seat was used for this project.)

Sandpaper, medium grit and 400 grit wet/dry sandpaper

Outdoor enamel or outdoor spray paint

Fast-drying polyurethane

2" paintbrush

Foam brushes

Fabric to fit seat

Batting or foam to fit seat

Floral or other images

White glue or decoupage medium

Acrylic spray (if using computer-printed images)

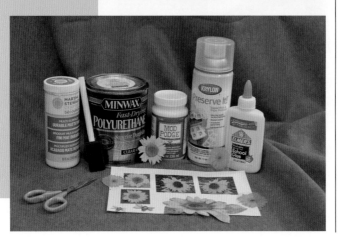

About Fabric and Batting

If your chair will be used only occasionally, cotton or cotton blend fabrics will do just fine. There is quite an array of colors and styles from which to choose at the fabric store. If your chair will get routine use, choose upholstery-weight fabric or vinyl for your seat covering.

Batting can be purchased by the yard and in varying thicknesses. Several layers of lightweight batting can be layered to the desired thickness. Foam may be substituted; however, it is the more expensive option.

About Glues and Sealants

Regular white glue may be used to affix images and as a seal coat for most decoupage projects. Producers of some decoupage media brands claim that they will produce a harder, more durable finish and may be a preferred option. As the chair will get some heavy use and could be exposed to heat and humidity, polyurethane should be used as the seal coat, rather than glue or decoupage medium.

About Images

This is the era of the paper crafter. Never before has there been such a huge selection of high-quality printed images for use in scrapbooking, card making, collage, and decoupage. In addition, there are special books that provide vintage and modern copyright-free images for your projects. This project goes one step further and shows you how to use photographs of your own garden to decorate the chair.

Precut shapes abound in the scrapbooking aisles of your craft store and online. Fresh pre-glued stickers will work just fine; older, dried-out ones will need to be affixed to your project with white glue or decoupage medium. Translucent stickers may not yield the results you want, as the colors will be less vibrant when placed onto your project.

1. Use medium grit sandpaper to remove loose paint and splintered wood from the chair. The amount of sanding needed depends on the condition of the chair and the quality of the final finish you desire. Re-sanding with fine sandpaper will result in a smoother finish that is preferable for a spray paint application.

There are scrapbook backer sheets that have some possibilities, and large sheets of images sold just for decoupage use.

2. Paint the chair with outdoor enamel. Recoat if necessary and let it cure for several days before continuing. (Or spray paint following the manufacturer's instructions.)

Any image can be scanned, enlarged, or shrunk, and printed with an inkjet or laser printer. These images must be sealed with a clear acrylic spray coating before use.

3. While the chair is drying, remove the seat from the chair, and remove any nails or tacks from the underside of the seat. Use the wood seat as a pattern to cut the batting the same size as the seat. Three layers were used here.

4. Use the seat as a pattern to cut the fabric the same size as the seat, plus 3" on all sides. Center the batting on the seat and the fabric on top of the batting. Hold all the layers together with one hand, and flip the seat over with the other.

5. Fold the fabric to the back on two opposite sides, then the other two sides. Staple the fabric to the seat in the center, about an inch from the edge. Move to the opposite side. Pull the fabric taut, but not too tight, and place a staple in the center, about one inch from the edge. Staple the third side, then move to the fourth side; pull the fabric taut, and staple it.

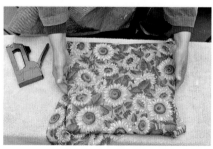

6. Flip the seat over to check that the fabric is not puckering anywhere. If it is, the fabric was pulled too tight and should be re-stapled. Continue to secure the fabric by placing staples several inches from the center staple on each side.

7. Make a crisp corner. Pinch the fabric together at the corner close to the seat. Squash the fabric arc in the center, with equal amounts of fabric on each side to form a kite shape.

8. Press the "kite" onto the seat and hold it firmly in place while stapling it to the seat.

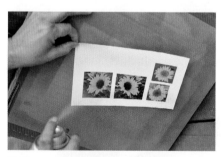

9. Prepare the images. Make your chair something special by using photographs of flowers from your own garden. Use a computer to place images on an 8$\frac{1}{2}$" x 11" page layout. Use the print setting—normal, high-quality, photo, etc.—that yields the best results. Print these out on regular copy paper. Let the images dry for thirty minutes, and then spray with a coat of clear acrylic. Allow it to dry for several hours.

10. Cut the images apart so that they are easier to work with. Scissors with 4" or 5" blades work best for delicate cutting. For best results, use long cutting strokes where possible, and cut the paper with the base of the blades, rather than the tips. An exception is with deeply incised areas, such as between the petals. Cut one side of the petal to the center, and then cut the other side to the center. The scrap should fall right off. If not, use the scissor tip to complete the cut.

11. Don't limit yourself to using the images exactly as they are. For example, the leaves on the right side of this flower were originally attached to the bottom. They were cut off and re-glued to the flower so that the piece would fit on the chair rail.

12. Use cellophane tape loops to position your images on the chair rails. Here several purchased images are on the top rail and the garden photos are on the bottom rail. Don't hesitate to add more images—vining plants, birds, butterflies, bunnies, watering cans, sunhats, and more can be combined to make your garden chair. When you are satisfied with the layout, remove the tape and set the images aside.

13. Pour some white glue or decoupage medium into a disposable bowl. Water it down a bit if necessary to make it more workable. Use a foam brush to apply a medium coat of glue in an area slightly larger than your image.

14. Place the image in water until the front and back become translucent. Pull it out and let the excess water drip off.

15. Place the image on the glued area and slide it into position. Use your fingers to lightly press out excess glue from the center outward. With a damp rag, press down all edges and corners of the image.

16. Gently wipe the image and surrounding areas with a slightly wet sponge to remove excess glue. Remove as much glue as you can from the chair, but don't wipe the image too much or you may damage it. Continue to glue the rest of your images onto the chair. Allow the glue to dry at least overnight. It may take

longer if the images you used were on thick paper.

17. If any portion of the image pops up while gluing or drying, use a paintbrush or toothpick to force the glue under the loose area. Press it down and remove any glue that squirted out with a damp rag.

18. Make sure that all edges of every image are completely glued and are flat. If not, now's the time to correct that. Once the glue is completely dry, apply a seal coat. If you use fast-drying polyurethane to seal the images, you should be able to recoat in about four hours, depending on the temperature and humidity. Check your product for precise information.

19. Use a foam or synthetic paintbrush to coat the entire chair rail, using long, lengthwise strokes. Let the polyurethane dry and apply a second coat.

20. Allow the second coat to dry and then use wet/dry sandpaper to wet sand the polyurethane.

Wet the paper in plain water and very lightly sand over the entire chair rail in the lengthwise direction. Wipe off the film that has formed with a rag.

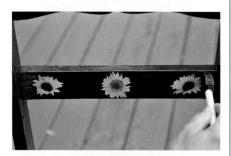

21. Apply three more coats of polyurethane, wet sanding between each coat to create a smooth finish. When you reach the last coat of polyurethane, you may want to coat the remainder of the chair so that the finish matches. Do not sand the final coat. Allow the chair to dry for several days before use. Pop on the seat and you are ready to offer a fancy chair to a party guest.

Those drab folding metal chairs just beg to be prettied up. Choose a color of outdoor aerosol paint to coordinate with your images. If the chair is rusty, for best results sand off all rust prior to painting. Two coats of paint were sprayed on this chair. Decoupage medium was used to glue the images onto the chair and five coats of medium were used on the images and the chair seat and back. The medium was wet sanded between coats as in the tutorial. Old rubber feet were replaced, and a new garden chair was created.

Painted floorcloths

Butterflies are self-propelled flowers.

George and Martha Washington's dining table at Mt. Vernon sat atop a checkered floorcloth which is still on display after two hundred years. Most of the preserved eighteenth-century homes of the well-to-do have at least one example of this once-popular art form. They were used as a substitute for very expensive carpets and area rugs. The blank floorcloth canvas offers the ultimate creative painting experience for crafters: simple to complex floral subjects, geometric shapes, abstract designs, realistic landscapes, still-life subjects, and more. This beginner project involves the nontraditional application of image transfers to expand the design possibilities.

EQUIPMENT

T-Square
Yardstick
Paint roller and tray
2" paintbrush
Artist's
paintbrushes—
various width flat
brushes (³/₈" to
1"), round brush
for flowers, and
optional liner
brush for stems
Glue gun

SUPPLIES

10-ounce cotton
duck canvas
fabric, 1 yard
Artist's gesso
Water-based latex
paint (Leftover
house paint may
be used.)
Acrylic paints —
Light "sky" blue
and a complementary dark blue;
yellow oxide; red; orange; yellow
green and dark green; Naples
yellow; and white (for optional
color mixing)
Glue sticks
Iron-on fabric sheets for inkjet
printer
Large foam stamps—sun, butterfly,
geometric shape, etc.
Clear acrylic spray paint with UV
protection
Brush-on water-based polyurethane
Container and utensil for mixing
gesso
4' x 6' tarp
Rags and paper towels
Disposable palette, such as paper
plates or bowls, for acrylic paint

About Floorcloth Material

The cotton duck fabric sold at sewing stores is the most affordable option and works well for this project. Heavier weight, pre-primed canvas is sold in many widths at art supply stores. In the how-to text, this fabric will be referred to as your canvas. Wrinkles can become permanent in duck cloth or canvas, so always roll the canvas onto a tube or lay it flat.

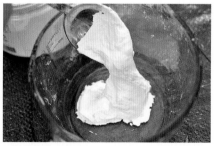

1. Gesso is a flexible primer used by artists to improve the ability of paint to adhere to canvas. Liquid gesso may be used straight from the bottle, while the gel-like gesso used here should be thinned with water to make it more workable. Spoon a generous amount of gesso into a cup or bowl.

2. Add a little water and stir with either a spoon or a wire whisk. Continue adding water a little at a time until the gesso reaches the consistency of latex paint. Water should not comprise more than 25 percent of your gesso mix. For example, 1 ounce of water mixed with 3 ounces of gesso is the maximum dilution rate.

3. Cut a 30" x 42" rectangle from the cotton duck fabric. Place it on the tarp and use a wide brush to apply the gesso to the entire surface. The canvas should remain flat while the gesso dries, which should be within a few hours, depending on the temperature and humidity. Apply a second coat of gesso, let the canvas dry completely, and then gesso the back side.

4. Pour some latex paint into a paint tray and use a roller to coat the entire canvas. Latex will take longer to dry than the gesso. Once it is completely dry, apply a second coat. Let the canvas dry thoroughly in a flat position, preferably overnight. Flip it over and apply one coat of latex to the back side. You may be surprised at how heavy the fabric has become.

5. To cut a perfect rectangle, do not measure from the edges. Rather, draw a rectangle in the center using a T-square. Start by placing the T-square about 2" in and roughly parallel to two sides. Draw a 36" line on the long edge of the T-square. Move the T-square to the end of the line you just made and place its edge on that line. Draw a 24" line. Move the T-square to the end of the 24" line and draw another 36" line. Line up the T-square again to draw the final 24" line.

6. The perfect rectangle will serve as your hem line. (A hemmed edge adds extra weight to help the floorcloth lay flat; however, a floorcloth may be made without a hem.) From the rectangle lines, add 1" all the way around for the cutting lines. To eliminate measuring errors, make at least three pencil marks along each line at the 1" mark. Place a straight edge so that it touches all three marks and draw a line. If only two marks line up, you've made a measuring mistake. Use sharp scissors to cut the canvas on the outer lines.

7. Trim the corners from the canvas in preparation for hemming. The cut should be an equal distance from each corner and should be made precisely at the corner of the hem line. If you prefer not to freehand cut this, make two marks that extend 2" in either direction from the corner. Draw a line from point to point. The line will just touch the point of the hem line.

8. Flip the canvas so that the back is facing up, and fold it to the inside along the hemline. Use your finger to press in a fold. The hem will not lie perfectly flat. The finger-pressed hem makes it possible to glue a straight hem. Glue the hem using a hot glue gun. Hot glue dries quickly, so you must work fast. Have a paper plate close by to rest the gun on as you work. Place a zigzag line on the 1" hem edge, starting with a short length. Use a rag to press the hem down onto the canvas to where the glue bead ends.

9. Continue to apply glue and press until the hem is complete.

10. Check all the hem edges, applying glue and pressing down any unglued sections. Wipe up any excess glue that squirts out.

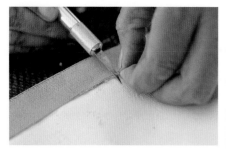

11. What should you do if you went overboard in the gluing process and have a thick line of glue on the edge of the hem? If it is still warm, try rubbing the glue gently in circles to remove it. If it is hard and cooled, use a craft knife to cut it from the canvas. Be very careful not to cut through the canvas.

12. Draw a border on the front of the canvas. To do so, measure and mark 1" from the edge all the way around and draw the outside border line. From that line, measure and mark 2" in and draw the inside border line.

13. Use a flat artist's brush to paint the border with blue acrylic paint.

14. Draw a 5" square block in each corner, offset $^1/2$" from the border edge. Measure in $1^1/2$" from the corner and draw two 5" lines. Measure $5^1/2$" in from the corner and complete the square.

15. Place a generous puddle of deep yellow oxide acrylic paint on a disposable palette. Start by painting the border of the square. Rather than painting a straight line, zigzag your line a bit. Pick up the brush at the end of each side and restart on the second side. If your corner is not crisply painted, use a damp paper towel to clean it up. Fill in the center of the square. Let the paint dry. If necessary, apply a second coat and let that dry.

16. Measure half the distance between two of the squares and make a mark along the top edge of the border. Repeat and place a mark on the bottom edge of the border. Then, measure half the distance between the bottom center mark you just made and the squares on each side. Make both marks on the bottom edge of the border. These need not be precise as they are just guidelines for placement of a flower stem.

17. Place puddles of yellow green and dark green on your palette. Use a narrow artist's brush or liner brush and the dark green paint to draw curving stems onto the border. Start at the middle of the square and draw a thin line toward the first mark on the border. Make an arc that flows to the center mark and then arcs back toward the third mark. Make a third arc that ends at the middle of the other square. Try to make the arcs fluidly in one long stroke. You can stop midway and pick up more paint if need be and then continue from that point.

18. Rinse the brush and wipe off with a paper towel. Pick up some light green and highlight one edge of the stem. When the paint dries you can touch up any areas that don't satisfy you, but don't be too concerned if the line gets wider in places. This will lend a natural, hand-painted look to your work.

19. Place an orange acrylic paint puddle on a palette. You can use a flat or round artist's brush to paint four- or five-petal flowers in the empty areas between the stems. Add a little

Naples yellow or white to lighten the orange. Paint over the still-wet petals to add some dimension. Allow the paint to dry and add a yellow center to each flower. Use yellow green and dark green paint to create two-toned leaves randomly along the stem and between some of the petals.

20. Paint the face of the sun stamp orange. Center it in the square and lower it onto the canvas. Press lightly on the entire stamp back, being careful not to slide the stamp. Lift the stamp straight up. Stamp the remaining three squares.

21. Use a 1" flat artist's brush to paint the background between the border light sky blue. If you accidentally get paint on the border, wipe it off with a damp paper towel. If it has already dried, touch it up with border paint. Allow the background paint to dry overnight.

22. Create the fabric appliqués. Use your computer to print photographs of butterflies (either photos you took or uncopyrighted images) onto a letter-sized page. Also on letter-sized paper, print an uncopyrighted border surrounding a quotation of your choice. The quotation used for this project is "Butterflies are self-propelled flowers."

23. Test print the butterfly image page and the quotation page, then print them on the iron-on fabric sheets using the manufacturer's recommendations for print settings. Let the sheets dry thirty minutes, and then cut out the images close to the edges.

The completed floorcloth.

24. Arrange the quotation block and the butterflies on the canvas. Measure and mark placement of your quotation block so that is straight when transferred to the canvas. Iron the quotation block and butterflies onto the canvas following the instructions that came with the material. Typically the instructions recommend using the cotton setting and no steam. It's a good idea to place a clean sheet of copy paper between the transfer and your iron to keep the transfer clean. Pay attention to pressing the edges well; they must be firmly adhered. Protect your canvas by brushing on two coats of water-based polyurethane.

Mini Bird Water Bowl
& candle dish

This dish does double duty: it supplies birds with a water source and provides a sturdy base for a pillar candle. This project sample uses gritty priming paint, soft sandy colors, and a couple of salamanders to add a bit of whimsy.

EQUIPMENT

Ruler or tape measure

SUPPLIES

8¹/₂" clay saucer
4¹/₂" clay pot (5¹/₂" tall)
Acrylic paints
Foam brush
Latex gloves
Clear matte finish acrylic spray
Latex-based masonry waterproofer*
Waterproof silicone adhesive
Super-type glue
Pencil
2 rubber toy salamanders
**Disposable palettes, such as paper
 plates or bowls**
*****If you want your project to have a
 smooth finish, substitute the latex-
 based sealer with a water-based
 one, such as H&C Concrete &
 Masonry Waterproofing Sealer.**

Check craft, toy, and dollar stores for offbeat items that will give your project a clever embellishment.

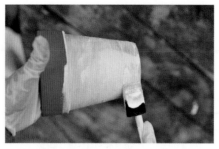

1. Wear protective gloves to apply a thick coat of latex-based masonry waterproofing paint to the top and bottom of the saucer and the outside, inside, and bottom of the pot. If you want to enhance the grittiness of this paint, you can mix in a small amount of craft sand. Prime the salamanders with a regular wood primer.

2. To make this project with a smooth finish, use an acrylic-based water-proofer to seal all surfaces of the pot and saucer. This product dries clear.

3. Make purple, yellow, and white paint puddles on a disposable palette. Mix a little yellow into the purple to make mauve pink. Apply this color in various places on the pot in uneven horizontal strips. The goal is to have several different values of the colors blended together.

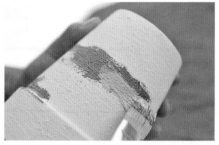

4. Add a little white to the mauve and mix it to form a light pink. Paint that color in between the darker colors, blending the edges as you go.

5. Add white to the yellow and continue painting. Be careful not to blend the paint too much. While you want the edges to be soft, you don't want the color blocks to become "muddy." If you're not happy with the results, let the paint dry and paint over it.

6. Paint the saucer with the same colors and in the same manner. Paint the salamanders to match or contrast with the pot.

7. Use one of the colors on your palette to paint the inside of the pot.

8. Calculate placement of the pot to the saucer by measuring the bottom diameter of each. Subtract the smaller number from the larger number and divide by two. In this case, it is 7" minus 3" equals 4", then 4" divided by 2" equals 2". Measure and mark 2" in from the saucer edge on four sides.

9. Apply a generous amount of silicone adhesive or carpenter's adhesive to the bottom of the pot. Use a craft stick to smooth out the adhesive to the edges.

10. Center the bottom of the pot using the centering marks. Use a tape measure or ruler to check in several places around the pot to make sure the pot is aligned properly. If not, adjust it and use a wet paper towel to clean up any glue that remains on the saucer.

11. Paint over the centering marks and allow the adhesive to dry.

12. Determine where to place the salamanders on the pot. Avoid painful mishaps by wearing gloves as you apply super-type glue to the salamander's body. Press the salamander in place, and hold for about fifteen seconds. Use a toothpick to dab some glue onto the salamander's feet and tail.

13. Position another salamander in the saucer with its head peeking out over the top edge. Glue the body, feet, and tail to the saucer.

14. Spray the entire piece with clear matte finish acrylic or polyurethane sealant. Allow the piece to cure for several weeks before filling it with water.

Make good use of that shell collection. Shells, fish netting, and driftwood are glued to the pot and saucer using tacky glue or waterproof PVA glue. I applied a clear acrylic-based water-proofer to the pot prior to painting. Three different shades of blue were blended to resemble Caribbean waters. Blue gems in the dish reflect the candlelight.

The candle was the inspiration for this desert scene. A small amount of craft sand was added to latex-based waterproofing paint to create a gritty desert feel to the piece. Saguaro cacti are silhouetted against a desert sunset.

Copper & Wood
wind chimes

In ancient times, wind chimes were believed to ward off evil. Eastern cultures have used them for centuries to rejuvenate the human mind and spirit. For farmers and sailors, chimes served the practical purpose of warning of an impending storm. While our project chimes are not tuned to produce a certain tone, the copper pipes deliver a rich, pleasant sound. The combination of copper and wood adds rustic visual charm to the garden.

EQUIPMENT

Hacksaw or pipe cutter
Drill with $1/8$" and $5/32$" bits
Vise
Hammer

SUPPLIES

Log slice—8" round and about $1/2$"
   thick
Hardwood disk for clapper—about
   $2^3/4$" across and 1" thick
Wind sail—piece of thick bark or
   wood stick
10' length of $3/4$" copper pipe
$1^1/4$" metal ring (key ring will work)
0000 steel wool
Nylon cord
Spar varnish
Foam brush
Thumbtack
Masking or cellophane tape
4 D common nail

1. On a protected surface, apply spar varnish to all surfaces of the log round, clapper and wind sail with a foam brush.

2. With a pipe cutter, cut the 10' copper pipe into the following lengths: 18", 16", 14", 12", and 10". (If you don't have a pipe cutter, place the pipe in a vise and cut with a hacksaw.) To use a cutter, place the pipe in the cutter channel and line up the blade to the cutting mark. Tighten the cutter by turning the hand knob until it is lightly pressed against the pipe. Rotate the tool around the pipe a turn or two. Continue tightening the knob a little bit at a time and rotating the tool until the cut is complete.

3. Rub a wad of #0000 steel wool along the length of each pipe to shine it up. If the copper is badly tarnished, you may want to consider using a liquid or paste copper cleaner and finishing it off with steel wool.

4. Place a mark 1" from the top edge of each of the copper pipes. Place each pipe in a vise, and use a $5/32$" drill bit to drill through the top side and then the bottom side of the pipe in one pass. Use a gloved finger or a small piece of steel wool to remove any burrs from the holes.

5. Center the wind chime hole template (which you can find on page 179) onto the log, tape it to the edge, and secure it in the center with a thumbtack. Hammer the common nail through the pattern at one of the marks, making about a ³/₈" deep indentation in the log round. Remove the nail, and repeat the process for the remaining marks.

6. Use a ¹/₈" drill bit to make holes at all of the indentations. Drill a center hole in the clapper round and a hole in the wind sail, close to its end.

7. Cut a 1¹/₂-yard length of nylon cord for the wind chime hanger and tape one end. The holes in the center circle are the hanger holes.

8. Thread the taped end of the cord down through one hole, leaving a 4" tail on the untaped end. (This tail remains on the top of the log round.) Bring this cord back up through the next closest hole.

9. Feed the taped cord end through the ring.

10. Feed the taped cord down through the next closest hole and then up again through the next hole. Lay the cord to the side.

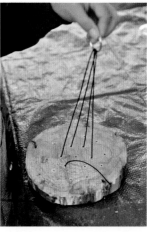

11. Hold the ring about 11" above the log round to extend the cord to the proper length. While holding the ring above the log round, thread the cord with the taped end through the ring and down through the next hole.

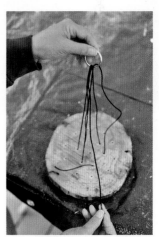

12. Feed the cord up through the fifth hole and through the ring. Even out all cords so that they are the same length.

13. Lay the ring and cords to the side. Tie a square knot close to the log round, using the cord with the taped end and the tail.

14. Cut the loose ends close to the knot, being careful not to cut through the hanging cords.

15. Threading the copper pipe uses the same process as the hanging cords. Cut two yards of nylon cord and tape one end. Hang the log round on a hook so that the pipes will swing freely as they are added. Thread the taped end through both holes in the 10" pipe.

16. With the pipe suspended from the cord, feed the taped end of the cord up through one hole in the log round and down through the next closest hole. Throughout this process, you will need to hold onto both ends of the cord, so leave enough cord on the tail end (which is on top of the log round) to do so.

17. At this point, it helps to have an extra set of hands to take the weight off the pipes as you are threading them on. Thread the taped end of the cord through both holes of the 12" pipe. Feed the taped end of the cord up through the next closest hole and down through the next hole. String the 14" pipe; feed the cord up and down. Do the same for the 16" and 18" pipes.

18. Firmly grip the two ends of the cord, which are both on top of the log round. Adjust all of the hanging cords so that the tops of the pipe are at the same level, about 5" down from the log round.

19. Tie a square knot close to the log round and trim the ends close to the knot.

20. Tie a double square knot on the end of a 1-yard length of nylon cord.

21. Tape the other end and feed it through the center hole from the top. Thread the taped end through the center hole of the clapper.

22. While holding the cord taut, position the clapper about 10" down from the top of the log round. Pinch the cord at the top of the clapper to mark knot placement. Pull off the clapper and tie a double square knot at your mark.

23. Restring the clapper and push it against the knot. Flip it over and tie a double square knot as close as possible to the clapper.

24. Thread the taped end of the cord through the wind sail and position it several inches below the longest pipe.

25. Your wind chimes are ready to serenade you. If your chimes do not sound when the breeze blows, you may need to replace either the clapper or the wind sail. Try using a harder wood for the clapper or cutting it slightly larger. The wind sail may need to be heavier, or it may need to be reshaped to catch more wind.

This chime is at home at the shore or wherever you want to be reminded of the sand and surf. Drill holes in a variety of shells as shown in the macramé tutorial (page 56). String the shells about 3" apart on thin hemp cord using an overhand knot. Here the cords are strung through the bottom of a basket. A bead tied at the end prevents the hanging cord from falling through the basket weave. No clapper is necessary; the shells will sing a song when they hit one another in the breeze.

Vine Trellis

Flowering vines provide vertical interest to a garden, especially a container garden. This lightweight version made from tomato stakes and natural jute is sized to support delicate vines in a 20" pot. You can use the same process to craft a sturdier version for the garden bed that will hold heavier plants. This trellis gives you a quick, easy, and inexpensive way to enjoy flowering vines and increase vegetable yields.

EQUIPMENT

Drill with ³/₈" and
    ¹/₄" bits
Wood saw
Screwdriver
Vise
Yardstick or tape measure

SUPPLIES

1" x 1" x 4' tomato stakes (3)
5 yards 3-ply 28# natural jute
    twine
1³/₄" deck screws (4)
1" wood beads (11)
Outdoor spray paint

1. Cut two 15" lengths from one of the stakes, starting at the top, flat end. Place the 15" section crosswise, flush with the end of the 4' stake, and draw a line. Do the same with the other 4' stake.

2. Line up the end of the yardstick to the line you drew and make marks every 5" down the length of the stake.

3. Place one of the 15" lengths cross-wise at the 30" mark (on the down side) and make lines on either side of the stake. Draw an "X" from corner to corner between the lines.

4. Use a ¹/₁₆" drill bit to drill a hole ³/₈" from the top and centered right to left.

5. Because the stakes are so narrow, it is helpful to drill ¹/₁₆" pilot holes at each 5" mark. At the 30" mark, drill the pilot hole in the center of the "X." Repeat Steps 4 and 5 with the other stake.

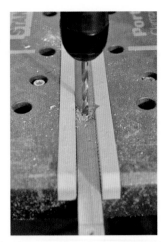

6. The first and last holes are ready to attach the wood crosspieces. Enlarge the five remaining pilot holes using a ¼" bit, but do not enlarge the top or bottom holes.

7. Drill a 1¾" deck screw through the top pilot hole in the 4' stake and into the end of the 15" cross-piece. Attach this crosspiece to the other 4' stake with a deck screw.

8. Use deck screws to attach the second crosspiece to both stakes at the 30" mark, drilling through the stakes and into the crosspieces.

9. Place the trellis on a protected surface and spray with classic white outdoor spray paint. This project offers a good way to use up leftover paint. You can use deck paint, stain, or outdoor enamel over a primer coat.

10. Cut five 20" lengths of the hemp twine. Use masking or cellophane tape to wrap each end. Insert one end of the twine through the top hole from the outside edge and through the corresponding hole on the other side.

11. Tie an overhand knot and push it close to the trellis frame, leaving a 4" tail. Do the same on the other side, pulling the hemp twine tightly so there is no slack.

12. Feed the twine through a bead and use an overhand knot to secure it. Repeat the process for the remaining horizontal supports.

13. Cut a 5' length of hemp twine and tape the ends. Feed one end through the top hole from the bottom to the top. Secure it with an overhand knot, leaving a 4" tail. Feed a bead onto the twine and tie another overhand knot to secure it.

14. Pull the twine down, loop it around the first horizontal twine, and tie a cross hand knot. Adjust it if necessary so that the vertical twine is taut.

15. Continue to tie on the vertical length of twine in the same manner.

16. Cut off the excess twine close to each bead.

17. Your trellis is ready for the planting season.

Grapevines also make great supports. Here a natural look is achieved by using grapevine instead of hemp twine. Waterproof carpenter's outdoor wood glue will help secure the stems.

Tropical
fountain

One thing that is commonly missing from deck and patio gardens is the relaxing sound of running water. While a pond may be impractical and too time consuming for the busy crafting gardener, this portable fountain is just the ticket. Trickling water flows down large leaves made from aluminum sheeting, creating a tropical paradise in a tub.

EQUIPMENT

Utility scissors
Stylus or pencil with dull point
Paper stomp tool or bone folder for
    paper crafting
Hacksaw

SUPPLIES

Plastic tub (about 18-gallon capacity)
    without drainage holes
Small fountain pump with flow
    control valve, about 150 gallons-
    per-minute flow
Tube of 36-gauge sheet aluminum
    (12" x 3')
Package of 3' bamboo poles
1-gallon plastic nursery pots (4)
Pea gravel to fill the nursery pots
Yard of 12-gauge residential
    electrical wire or similar
Roll of adhesive-backed 2" metal foil
    tape
Can of leaf green spray paint
4' length of clear flexible tubing that
    fits your pump nozzle
Faux tropical houseplant stems to fill
    in between fountain leaves
9" x 12" sheet of crafter's foam

1. You can use the tub as is or cover it with wallpaper or fabric. This tub is wrapped with light green burlap and embellished with cattail leaf and spike silhouettes made from dark brown burlap. Cut the burlap to fit your container, allowing a couple of inches to overlap at the seam and to tuck under the bottom. Use spray adhesive to attach the burlap to the container, smoothing out wrinkles as you go. If need be, slice the burlap where there are protrusions on the pot and press the burlap around them.

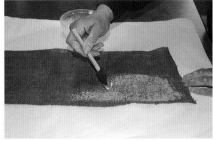

2. Thin white glue with a little water to make it more spreadable. Use a foam brush to coat one side of a strip of burlap that's long enough to accommodate the cattail spikes. This will prevent the burlap from fraying when it is cut.

3. Trace cattail leaves and spikes on paper and cut them out. Place the shapes on the burlap, trace around the edges and cut them out, or freehand draw the leaves directly onto the burlap.

4. Attach the cattail leaves and spikes to the burlap using spray adhesive or white glue. Seal coat the burlap with outdoor silicone water shield spray.

5. Make a paper pattern of a leaf that is about 11" wide and 16" long. Place the foil on a hard, smooth surface, such as a metal tray or marble piece. Use a metal tooling stylus or a dull pencil point to trace your pattern or freehand draw a long, wide leaf shape on a sheet of craft aluminum. Cut out the shape with utility scissors.

8. Cut into the leaf about $1/4$" to $3/8$" deep at the center of the bottom and tip of the leaf. Make $1/4$" to $3/8$" cuts from the edge inward along the entire edge of the leaf about $1^1/2$" apart. Make these cuts anywhere between the leaf veins.

11. Attach an 18" length of 12-gauge electrical wire to the bottom of the leaf using a 12" strip of aluminum foil tape. About 5" of wire should extend from the bottom of the leaf. Press the tape down firmly on either side of the wire.

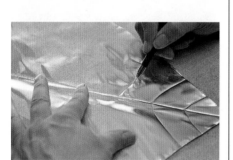

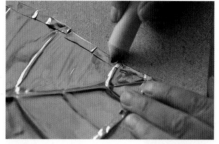

6. Run the stylus along a straight edge from tip to tip to add the center leaf vein. Create side veins by drawing from the center vein to the edge. Space the veins closer together as you near the leaf tip.

9. Fold the aluminum under to the end of each cut and press it down. Each section should be folded to where the cut meets the metal leaf. Smooth out any angular edges to form a smooth leaf edge. Use the stomp or bone folder to burnish the edges flat.

12. Place the end of a bamboo pole where the wire emerges from the leaf. Wrap with green duct tape from this point down the pole until the wire is covered.

7. Flip the leaf to the back side and place it on a sheet of crafter's foam. Accentuate the main and side veins with the stomp or bone folder. Use a back and forth scribbling motion to press the aluminum from the center to the edge of each vein.

10. Flip the leaf over and check the edge. If you have a metal spur, correct it by pulling up the metal strip which is not folded properly. Replace it so that it is folded where the cut meets the leaf. Re-burnish the edge.

13. Make two additional leaves the same size as the first, and fasten them to bamboo poles. Additional smaller leaves can be made to fill in the leaf arrangement and hide tape seams. Spray paint the front and back sides of the leaves using spray paint for plastic.

14. Position your fountain where you plan to use it. Once it is filled with water, it will be very heavy to move. Fill four 1-gallon nursery pots with pea gravel and place them in the tub, along the outer edge.

15. Wrap the length of tubing with green duct tape.

16. Set the pump on the lowest flow setting, attach the tubing, and place it securely on the bottom of the tub with the suction cups.

17. Place each bamboo pole in a separate nursery pot so that the pole is touching the bottom of the pot. Place the fourth pot toward the front of the tub. Bend each leaf slightly at the center vein so that it is not perfectly flat. Arrange the leaves so that the water will flow from the top leaf, spill onto the middle leaf, then onto the bottom leaf, and then into the tub. Shuffle the pots around as necessary. Use a hacksaw to cut the bamboo poles to the proper heights.

18. Test the water flow by holding the tube at the stem end of the highest leaf and turning on the pump. The water should just flow onto each leaf without splashing. Once you are satisfied, curl the tubing loosely around the bamboo pole which supports the top leaf. Tape it to the pole so that the opening is properly placed for water to flow onto the leaf. For added security, drive a 1⅝" deck screw through the tube into the bamboo pole.

19. Place stems of faux tropical leaves into the fourth pot to make the fountain look lush and to hide the pots. Use duct tape to affix leaves where they will disguise duct-taped joints and rope handles. Add stems to the other three pots to fill them out.

20. Add water to the tub, adjust the leaves as needed, and plug in the pump. The water in the tub can evaporate fairly quickly on a hot, sunny day, so be sure to keep the tub filled with enough water to at least cover the pump. Never let the pump run without water.

Adorn
the walls

Leaf-Printed
outdoor wall art

One thing that is often missing from outdoor living areas is artwork. Even if you are not an experienced painter, you can create one-of-a-kind art using the leaf-print technique. With proper preparation and sealing, this artwork will resist damage by rain and sun. Grab a brush and a beret and get ready to create your own outdoor art gallery.

EQUIPMENT

Surface protector, such as drop cloth or tarp
Artist's paintbrushes
Tack hammer

SUPPLIES

Stretched artist's canvas (18" x 18" was used in this project)
Paper or foam plates
Paper towels
Water-filled disposable cup
Acrylic paints of your choice (cerulean blue, oxide of chromium, phthalo blue, light green, ultramarine blue, alizarin crimson, yellow, and white were used in this project)
Acrylic spray sealant with UV protection
Saw tooth picture hanger
Large plant leaves— *Hosta* and *Canna* were used in this project

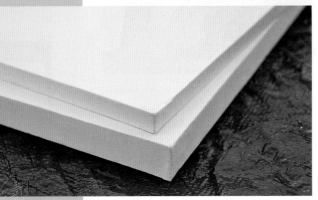

Selecting Acrylic Paints

Outdoor urban wall murals last for years thanks to the composition of acrylic paints. They bond well to most surfaces and are lightfast and weather resistant. (Note that cadmium colors and fluorescent paints are most likely to fade in direct sun.) Their fast-drying nature is a plus and a minus. It's a benefit when you need a layer to dry before proceeding. It's a detriment when, as you'll see in the tutorial, the paint dries too fast to be applied properly. Use the colors you like and have fun experimenting with color mixing.

Selecting Canvases

Choose a canvas that has been stapled to wood stretcher strips. Most of these canvases have already been primed with gesso, which makes the canvas more durable and helps the paint better adhere to the surface. A standard canvas is 1" deep or less. More costly museum or gallery canvases are generally meant to be hung without a frame and are 2" to $2^1/_2$" deep. Either type will work.

1. Prepare your palette by making puddles of the colors you plan to use. Charts and wheels are readily available to guide you in precise color mixing. You'll discover that you can get the colors you want with a little experimentation. Add yellow to dark green until you achieve a color you like. Add white to make a lighter tint of the same color. Combining yellow and blue results in green. Blue added to green in varying amounts makes a teal. Add alizarin crimson to green to darken it. (Resist using straight black; just a little overpowers other colors.) Want a grayed or dusky color? Make gray by combining ultramarine blue and brown umber. Add white until you get the intensity you want. Then mix in a little green or blue. Have a container of water close by so that you can rinse your brush and wipe it with a paper towel when changing colors.

2. Create a background by loosely painting on blocks and swipes of paint from your paint palette. (It may help to look at the final canvas in Step 9 to see what the goal is.) To keep it simple, use only three or four different colors, and then accent the piece with one or two other colors. In this version, the accent colors are a light yellow-green and a strong teal blue-green. Work wet on wet, blending the edges together for a softer look. You don't want to repeatedly paint over another color or you could get a muddy appearance. Continue to pick up paint from the palette, cleaning your brush as you change colors and filling in large areas of canvas.

3. Bright yellow-green highlights are placed randomly around the canvas. Teal highlights are used sparingly.

4. Since the painting won't be framed, the side edges will be visible. While the canvas is still wet, paint the edges in the same manner as the front. Allow the background paint to dry thoroughly. In normal humidity, this should take only a few hours.

5. Cut an assortment of *Canna, Hosta*, and other leaves of varying sizes, along with several inches of stem. Place the leaves on the canvas in a pleasing arrangement: overlap them, place them at different angles, and consider folding a leaf or two in half.

6. Set up a fresh palette with colors for the leaves. This one includes two greens, teal (blue-green), red, yellow, and bright aqua blue. Once you practice this technique, you may decide to use non-traditional leaf and background colors such as bright orange or purple. If you don't like your creation, you can wipe most of the paint off with a paper towel and repaint, or let it dry and paint over it. Experiment with mixing paint to create new colors, as you did for the background.

7. Place a leaf on a paper towel or newspaper with the vein side facing upward. Apply a fairly thick layer of one color, brushing from the center vein to the edge of the leaf.

8. Add lighter green colors to the leaf, blending them with the base color.

9. Red painted on the stem and in selected spots adds some interest.

10. Once the entire leaf is painted and you are satisfied with the results, carefully pick it up and flip it over. You cannot reposition the leaf once it is pressed onto the canvas, so do your best to place it exactly where you want it. Press the entire leaf surface lightly to transfer the paint to the canvas.

11. Pick up the leaf by the stem and pull it slowly off from bottom to top.

12. This impression yielded disappointing results. Because the project was created outside on a hot day and the leaf was so large, the acrylic paint began to dry before it could be completed.

13. If this happens, don't despair. Just pick up your brush and fill in the gaps with some matching paint. Allow the canvas to dry before proceeding to the next leaf.

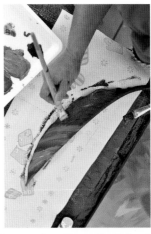

14. Next up is a *Canna* leaf that is folded in half. Remember that you want to paint the back side that contains the veining. A blend of dark and light greens forms the base layer, with dark red and bright blue highlights.

15. Place the leaf precisely where you want it on the canvas. Use your bare hand or a paper towel to press lightly on the leaf to transfer the paint to the canvas.

16. Pull it off slowly from the stem to the top. If you want to make any adjustments, pick up your brush and do so. If you are happy with the results, let the canvas dry and move on to the next leaf.

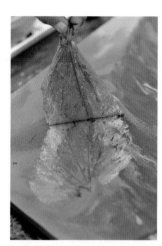

17. This large leaf of a Dragon Wing *Begonia* will brighten up the canvas when painted with a green center and yellow margin.

18. The final leaf is a medium *Hosta* leaf painted dark green with yellow margins and a touch of dark red highlights. Treat it the same as the others: paint, position, press, and remove.

19. Some artists like unplanned random streaks and paint blotches that sometimes just happen as part of the process. If you don't like the way something looks, pick up the brush and paint it over. Just be mindful that you don't want to repaint the background one solid color. Use several colors and blend as you go to match the surrounding background.

20. After the paint has thoroughly dried, the final step is to sign your work. Thin out some paint with a small amount of water and use a fine liner brush to paint your name or initials in one of the lower corners. Flip the canvas over and place it on a clean newspaper or tarp. Paint the wood stretcher any solid color that matches your painting.

21. Once the back is completely dry, spray several coats of acrylic sealer on the front and back of the painting using sweeping motions. Use a clear coat that includes a UV ray protector to offer added protection from fading.

22. After the seal coat dries, place the painting face down on a clean surface and find the center of the top. Center a saw tooth picture hanger over the mark and use a tack hammer to tap the points into place.

23. Your masterpiece is ready to put on display. The artwork will last for many years if it is hung undercover, but it should hold up to several summer seasons through inclement weather.

Here, solid chartreuse was painted on the canvas and allowed to dry thoroughly. Fresh fern leaves were sprayed with adhesive and positioned on the canvas. Regular dark green spray paint was applied all over in a sweeping motion. The fern leaves were removed, revealing an interesting piece of garden art.

Solid colors also make good backgrounds for printing *Canna* leaves.

A black background is a dramatic choice to showcase this large *Hosta* leaf.

Clay Wall
pocket planters

There are good reasons art teachers and camp counselors use clay: it's fun to work with, and students can achieve good results without having any art training or experience with the medium. If you haven't worked with clay since you were a kid, give this project a try. You do not need to fire your piece in a kiln, as with earthen clay pieces, and this wall pocket design is ideal for beginners.

EQUIPMENT

Plastic to protect work surface

Canvas drop cloth or cotton fabric, about 2' x 2'

Large kitchen knife

Butter knife or plastic knife

Rolling pin

Latex or vinyl gloves

Drinking straw or pencil

Foam brushes

Artist's brushes

Section of tree bark with deep indentations

Water bowl

Drying rack

Wire cutter

SUPPLIES

Air drying, self-hardening clay (One 5-pound box will make one large wall pocket)

Waterproofing sealant

Water-based sealant

Acrylic paints—white, ultramarine blue, burnt umber, Naples yellow, copper (optional)

8" length of coated wire (Any flexible cord may be used as long as it will not rot.)

Selecting Clay

The type of clay used for this project is air drying, *self-hardening* clay. For this project, Amaco Self-Hardening Mexican Pottery Clay was used. (Do not use plain air-drying clay. The finished project is likely to crumble and the joints separate.) Other brands are suitable, but will differ in moisture content, workability and weight. The DAP brand, for example, is softer and gummier to use and the finished product is much lighter than that made with Mexican Pottery Clay. Experiment to find the brand of clay you like to work with. Note that instructions for this type of clay will say that finished pieces are not waterproof. This wall pocket is not intended to hold water as a vase. Once waterproofed, painted, and sealed, the piece

will become quite water resistant and should hold up for many seasons as a planter. Check the drainage hole periodically to ensure that it is not blocked. If you don't want to take a chance, use the pocket for dried or silk stems and keep it under cover.

Waterproofers, Paints, and Sealants

For this project, H&C Concrete & Masonry Waterproofing Sealer, Helmsman Spar Varnish and tube acrylic paints were used, but other brands are suitable. Follow label directions on the brands you use.

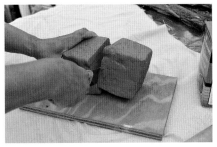

1. Prepare your work surface by placing the canvas or cotton cloth over a sheet of plastic. Place your equipment within easy reach. Unwrap the clay and place it on a cutting board. Use the kitchen knife to cut the block in half. Cut one of the halves in half again.

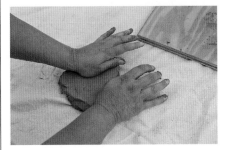

2. Kneading the clay a bit will make it more pliable and easier to work with. Take about a minute to stretch out the edges, fold them into the center, and reform the ball, rolling it between your hands. Place the kneaded clay on the cloth and flatten it using the heels of your hands.

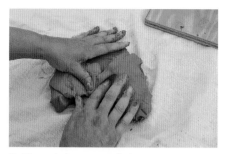

3. Knead the second clay quarter as you did with the first. Place the kneaded clay on top of the flattened clay disk and combine the two.

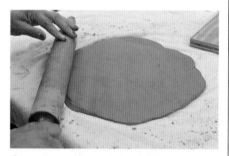

4. With a rolling pin, start from the center of the disk and roll outward, using even pressure from the center to the edges. Roll a circle about 12" round and an even thickness. The surface should be smooth, with no deep cracks. If it isn't, ball the clay again and reroll it if necessary.

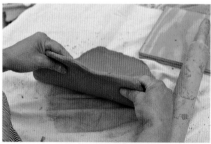

5. Pick up one edge of the clay circle and check for thickness. It should be between $1/4$" and $3/8$" thick.

6. Slice the remaining clay block in half. Knead each quarter separately as before. Combine the two quarters and roll out as in Steps 4 and 5. Check to see that the edges are between $1/4$" and $3/8$" thick. Reroll if necessary to achieve a smooth, crack-free surface.

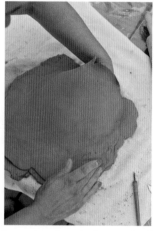

7. Pick up the clay circle you had set aside and place it over the other circle. Do not worry about matching the edges perfectly as they will be sliced off. Support the center of the circle with one hand and lightly press the edges of the two clay circles together on one side. While still supporting the center, lightly press the edges of the other side and bottom together. Once positioned, use firm pressure to mesh the two edges of the clay together around the sides and bottom edges. Continue to support the center while doing this.

8. Use the butter knife, plastic knife or other cutting tool to slice off the outer edges of the clay in the general shape of the wall pocket. Start at the top of one side and smoothly cut to the middle of the bottom edge. Pull off the excess clay on the cut edge. This will give you a clear look at the shape when you cut the second side.

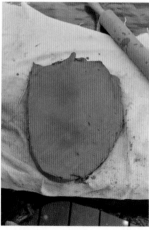

9. Start at the top of the second side, and use the same smooth motion to trim off the excess clay. Support the pocket with one hand if it helps you to visually match the side you are cutting with the other side of the pot. As this is a free-form wall pocket, do not be concerned if the two sides are not perfectly symmetrical. Remove the excess clay from the second side. Do not be concerned about the uneven top edge or irregular side edges.

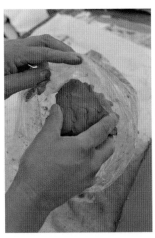

10. Before continuing, place the remaining clay in its original plastic bag, seal it, and put in into the box. If you don't plan to use the clay right away, it's a good idea to wrap the clay ball in kitchen plastic wrap, place it in the bag, and then into an airtight plastic container.

11. Lift off the top sheet of clay, move the bottom out of the way, and place the top on your work surface.

12. Imprint or stamp the clay pocket by laying the bark piece onto the clay with the indentations running vertically and pressing down firmly. Continue to work your way across the pocket, overlapping and with the bark in the same vertical orientation.

Mending Holes & Building Up Thin Areas

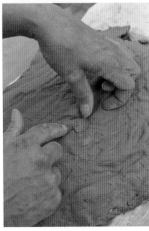

Mend any holes or thin areas that appear by placing a generous amount of clay over the area and re-stamping it with the bark. It is preferable to have an area that may be thicker than the overall pocket, rather than have a wall that is too thin.

1. Use the knife to even up the top of the pocket. Do not be too precise with your cut; indentations and snags will make your piece look more realistic. Using a small piece of bark, stamp along the entire top edge of the pocket. Set this piece aside.

2. Sign your work. Pick up the back clay section of the wall pocket. Dip your hand in the water bowl and wet the area where you want to place your mark. Use a bamboo skewer, stylus, or other similar tool to inscribe your name or initials. You could also make an imprint with a rubber stamp.

3. Gently place the wall pocket on your work surface with the signed side down.

4. Position the imprinted front section of the wall pocket over the back so that the edges meet. Press the edges together firmly on three sides.

5. Make a final trim cut.

6. Place your hand inside the pocket to check that all edges are firmly pressed together. Lift the pocket and adjust it so that it is not leaning to one side.

7. Use the small piece of bark to imprint the wall pocket back. Keep the bark indentations running vertically. Reinforce the joint where the wall pocket edges meet at the top by adding a small amount of clay and squeezing together to ensure a good bond. Imprint the edge area with the small piece of bark.

8. Use a ruler to find the center of the pot, where the hanging holes will be placed. Make marks 1" to the left and right of the center. With the drinking straw, pencil, or other tool, make a hole at each mark.

9. Find the center of the bottom and make a drainage hole. Be sure the hole clears the bottom of the back side of the wall pocket.

10. Gently pick up the wall pocket and place it on the drying rack. Make any adjustments to the piece at this time. Lift the pocket into its correct position. Be sure that the entire bottom section is lying flat on the rack. The pocket should remain in the shape you created. If it sags, that may indicate that your pocket walls were not thick enough. Support a sagging pocket by inserting crumpled up newspaper or bubble wrap. Do not use a solid object as a support, as your clay piece will shrink as it dries. If the clay is prevented from shrinking, it will crack.

Place the drying rack in a warm room, out of direct heat and sun. The clay will lighten in color as it dries.

The clay must be thoroughly dry before you proceed. This may take a week, or longer if you have placed support material in the pocket. You should remove the support material after a day or so to allow air to reach the inside.

11. Wear protective gloves for the waterproofing steps. Pour waterproofing sealant in a disposable bowl and use a foam brush to thoroughly coat the outside of the wall pocket. Be sure the solution gets into all of the bark indentations.

12. Coat the inside of the pocket, being careful to not miss any areas. (It is normal for the brush to pick up some of the clay color.)

13. Tilt the pocket and coat the bottom.

14. Place the wall pocket on the drying rack and allow it to thoroughly dry. This may take up to forty-eight hours.

15. Now it's time to finish your wall pocket. To achieve the most natural results, use several colors to paint your wall pocket. Trees may be predominantly brown, gray, or red, but they are actually a combination of different values and hues. This project uses burnt umber, medium brown, and Naples yellow, with copper as a highlight. Black is mixed with white to make gray. A nice gray can also be made by mixing ultramarine blue and burnt umber; add white to achieve different values of gray. Brush on the various colors while the paint is wet, and blend them for a natural look. You do not need to switch brushes between colors. Just swish the brush in a cup of water and wipe the bristles with a paper towel.

16. Start by painting shadows in the nooks and deep indentations with black paint.

17. Apply the medium brown and burnt umber randomly over the pocket. Add touches of Naples yellow on the higher ridges to add some highlights. Soften the edges of the highlighted areas and the edges of the black shadowed areas.

18. If you blend too much and end up with one solid color, wipe off most of the wet paint with a paper towel, let the piece dry, and start over. The piece should be dry and workable in an hour or so.

19. Copper highlighting is applied sparingly on several of the high bark ridges.

20. Paint the bark on the back piece to match the pocket, going a bit lower than the soil line will be.

21. The inside of the pocket won't be viewed once the pocket is planted, but paint it with burnt umber, medium brown, or another color of your choice. Be sure not to miss any spots.

22. Let the paint dry, then paint the back burnt umber, medium brown, or a color of your choice.

23. Even though the paint will feel dry to the touch in a few hours, let the wall pocket dry for at least forty-eight hours. Check the inside of the pocket to be sure the paint is completely dry before proceeding.

24. Use a sponge brush to apply the seal coat. The manufacturer of this clay recommends shellac or varnish, although polyurethane will also work. Brush out any puddles and wipe up drips as you go. You can save time if you rig a dowel to a board to support the wall pocket as it dries. I used an old-style napkin holder repurposed as a drying peg. Otherwise, use a drying rack that is placed on newspaper. Coat the inside and outside of the pocket, and allow it to dry thoroughly. Flip it over, coat the back, and allow the back to dry. Reposition so that it does not touch the newspaper during the drying time.

25. Insert the end of a 6" length of coated wire from the back through one of the hanger holes and down through the other.

26. Even up the ends and tie a square knot by crossing the right end over the left, then the left end over the right. Pull it tight so that there is about 1¹/₂" from the pot to the knot on both sides.

27. Wrap the loose ends three or four times around the secure wire on both sides. Cut off any excess.

28. Your wall pocket is ready for you to add lightweight potting mix and a plant. Hang the planter securely in the sun or shade, depending on the needs of your plant.

Wall pockets were immensely popular from the 1920s through the 1950s. Animals, flowers, food, and human faces were common designs. In addition to holding live plants, pockets may be used to display dried and silk flower arrangements. This bird's nest pocket was made by forming the clay pocket as in the tutorial. Thin strands of clay were made with an extruder tool, commonly sold with the polymer clay products at craft stores and online. The strands were carefully laid onto the pocket and gently pressed down on the sides. Several small branches were made by rolling a snake of clay between the palms. The branches were intermingled with the strands for a realistic look of a bird's nest. After drying thoroughly, the piece was coated with waterproofing sealant, painted with acrylic paints, and finished with spar varnish. A note of caution: this piece is very delicate, especially before it is painted and finished. This wall pocket is the perfect vessel for a collection of bird feathers.

Garden
reflections

Add an unexpected touch to your outdoor entertaining area or garden. In the shade, a mirror supplies a flash of light where it's most needed. In the sun, it makes light dance and sparkle. Properly placed, a mirror will reflect the garden beyond your deck or patio. This project uses smooth, subtly colored river rocks to form an organic art piece.

EQUIPMENT

Caulking gun

Wide putty knife

Yardstick or ruler

Pencil

Nail

Phillips screwdriver

Jigsaw

SUPPLIES

Paper or painting canvas for pattern

18" x 24" plywood board

Deck stain (primer and acrylic or latex paint may be substituted)

12" x 12" mirror

12" x 12" cardboard

Painter's tape or wide masking tape

Large (about 1$1/2$" to 2") smooth rocks in various colors

Medium (1" to 1$1/2$") smooth rocks in various colors

Small ($1/2$" to 1") smooth rocks in various colors

Tube of construction adhesive

Tube of clear silicone tub and tile caulk

Heavy duty picture hanging kit

Selecting River Rocks

The most economical way to purchase smooth rocks is in $1/2$ cubic-foot bags at the hardware or big box store or from a hardscape supplier. Called river rocks or smooth rocks, they are available in several mixed color assortments. Most of these stores also sell smaller bags of decorative rocks. The advantage to the smaller, pricier bags is that the rocks are sorted by color and size.

To make the mirror as shown you will need approximately one dozen large rocks, three dozen medium gray rocks, four dozen medium white rocks, ten dozen small rocks of various colors for the medallions, four dozen small white rocks for filler, and twenty dozen black rocks for filler.

If you buy a large bag, you will first need to sort the rocks by color and size. Once you start creating your design, you'll see if you have a sufficient supply of each color.

1. Create your design. A large sheet of paper will work, but an artist's stretched canvas is the perfect base to form your pattern, as it is easy to move out of the way if necessary. Determine the size of your piece based on the size and shape of the mirror. The mirror does not have to be centered, nor does it have to be a typical shape. A nice shard from a broken mirror could make an interesting free-form piece. Draw your design on the paper/canvas. In this 18" x 24" piece, a 3" border surrounds the 12" mirror. The top features a large center medallion and sloping edges.

Start placing rocks directly on the paper/canvas and move them around until you are satisfied.

2. Cut a piece of $1/2$" plywood to the size of your design, using a jigsaw to shape the edges. Paint both sides of the frame to coordinate with your design. If you use deck paint or stain, there is no need to prime the wood before painting. Prime if you are using latex or acrylic paint.

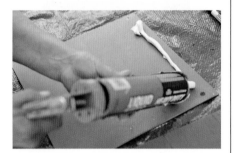

3. Transfer the pattern onto the frame. Here, lines indicate the mirror placement and a surrounding 3" border.

4. With a caulking gun, apply a generous amount of adhesive to the back of the mirror.

5. Use a wide putty knife to spread the adhesive evenly over the entire surface up to the edges.

6. Flip the mirror over and place it on the guidelines marked on the frame.

7. A damp paper towel will clean up any adhesive that is on the mirror. Protect the mirror by affixing a piece of cardboard with painter's tape or masking tape.

8. Place your pattern next to the frame so that you can begin transferring rocks to the frame.

9. Apply a generous amount of silicone adhesive to the backs of the large rocks that will form the centers of the medallions. Press each rock firmly in place.

10. The medium white rocks that form the border of the mirror are placed snugly against the mirror and each other.

11. To complete the medallions, squeeze a generous amount of adhesive directly onto the frame around each center rock and attach the smaller rocks.

12. Work the frame between medallions by applying a generous amount of adhesive to the frame in small sections. Carefully select black rocks to fit snugly around the border and around the large rocks. Note that at this point you can still slide the rocks around and remove them if they're not a good fit.

13. This process will probably take a little more time than you expect. You may discover that it is a good after-work stress reliever. Between crafting sessions, be sure to recap the adhesive tube tightly and place your frame and pattern out of the elements.

14. After all the rocks are adhered to the frame, let the adhesive dry for several days. Carefully flip the frame over onto a firm surface. Measure the length of the frame and divide that number by three, then use that figure to place a chalk or pencil mark one-third down from the top.

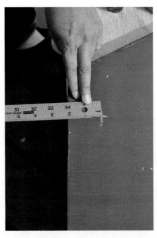

15. Measure in 2" from the sides and make a cross where the two points meet.

16. Place the hanger so that the top is at the cross mark. Use a pencil or permanent marker to indicate where the screw holes should be placed. Hammer a common nail into the frame at each mark and then pull it out. These will serve as pilot holes for the hanger screws.

17. Use the appropriate size Phillips screwdriver to attach the hangers.

18. The length of hanger wire you will need is the distance between the hangers, plus several inches on each side and several more inches to serve as slack. When pulled taut, the hanger wire should fall a couple of inches down from the top of the frame so that your wall hanger is not visible once the frame is hung.

19. Insert one side of the wire into the hanger loop, leaving a 3" tail. Wrap the tail around the hanger wire. Repeat for the other side.

20. Flip the frame over and remove the tape from the mirror. If you pull slowly with even pressure, and without angling the tape, it should come off in one piece.

21. Polish the mirror and your masterpiece is ready for display. It's advisable to store the mirror inside or under cover if your climate is harsh during the winter months. This mirror, however, was subjected to rain and snow through a northeastern winter to test the adhesives and was not damaged.

Mirrors will brighten up shady spots and can provide a colorful view in a sitting area. Holes were drilled into the metal trellis and mirror clips were used to attach a large round mirror. Over time, water and humidity will deteriorate the silver oxide coating on the back of the mirror. When that happens, you can either replace the mirror or enjoy its antique appearance.

Mirrors can brighten up seasonal wreaths. The base is a 13" gold charger—a decorative plate that is available in metallic colors at craft and home stores. An 8" round mirror was glued in the center with silicone tub and tile adhesive. The stems were affixed with 1/4" clear florist's tape, which makes it easy to remove them and create another design. Hot glue can also be used for a more permanent piece.

Moss & Mushroom
wreath

This wreath evokes sights, sounds, and smells of a spring walk in the woodland. The secret ingredient is moss, which gives any project an organic look and feel. Preserved moss comes in a variety of green, blue, and gray shades, and will retain its color for decades if kept out of direct sun. One word of warning—once you start mossing things up, you may not be able to stop! You are sure to find a multitude of ways to embellish other garden craft projects with this natural element.

EQUIPMENT

**High- or low-temperature glue gun
with compatible glue sticks**

Wire cutters

SUPPLIES

18" straw wreath form

**Preserved thick sheet moss (about 22
ounces to cover an 18" wreath)**

**Assortment of preserved loose
mosses**

Dried mushrooms

Tree branch, about 8" in length

**Variety of assorted botanicals,
including seed pods, branch tips,
dried fern fronds, and flowers
(optional)**

Artificial small-leaved ivy vines

Florist's 26-gauge green paddle wire

Florist's picks with wire

Florist's "U" pins

About Glue Guns

There are low-temperature, high-temperature and dual-temperature glue guns. The low-temp melts glue at about 250 degrees, and the high-temp melts glue at about 380 degrees. Glue sticks are made to match the temperature you are using. Either one can result in a skin burn, so take extra care when using these tools and do not allow children near them. Glue guns drip, so place a piece of paper or cardboard under the tip when you set it down.

Low-temp glue is a good adhesive for lightweight craft projects and materials such as paper, thin fabrics, and foam. High-temp glue has more holding power for items made of wood, plastic, and metal. A low-temp gun may be used to make this wreath. If you are impatient or work fast, however, you may prefer to use a high-temp gun. High-temp is especially useful when applying glue to large surface areas, as you'll get more liquefied glue per trigger pull.

1. Make the hanging loop. Wrap the florist's wire around the wreath form two times. Leave about 2" of slack between the wire and wreath frame. Cut the wire, leaving two 3"tails.

2. Wind the two tails around one another.

3. Wrap the wound tail around both of the wires that encircle the wreath. Form a loop by twisting the wire together close to the wreath form. Make the loop easy to find after the moss is applied by tying a twist tie or ribbon to it.

4. Cover the wreath form with palm-sized pieces of sheet moss. Large pieces are easily torn apart. Run lines of glue on the edges and center, place moss on the wreath form, and press the center and edges to ensure an all-over bond. If the glue is too hot for your fingers, use a wadded up paper towel or rag to press the moss.

5. Glue another piece of moss and butt it up against the first piece. Press it down as before. No straw should be showing through the moss segments.

6. If you discover an edge that was not completely glued down, run a line of glue between the moss and straw form. Chances are some glue will squirt out from under the moss, so use a paper towel or rag to press down the moss at these joints.

7. Continue to apply sections of moss until the entire wreath is covered.

8. Assemble your decorative materials and create an arrangement. Achieve a pleasing, natural look by layering items and not placing them symmetrically. Move the items off the wreath close to where they will be placed.

9. Attach the largest items first. If the dried mushroom is already attached to a wood stick, grasp the mushroom and the stick and push it into the wreath at an angle.

10. If the dried mushroom does not have a stick, insert both points of a florist's "U" pin into it close to the edge. Push the "U" pin firmly into the straw wreath form

11. Wrap wire around the stick and the wreath form and twist the two ends together close to the form. Cut the wire, leaving a 3" tail. Twist the two ends together and tuck under the wire.

12. Push the stem of a dried fern frond under one of the mushrooms and pin it to the wreath form using a "U" pin. Cut the stem close to the pin. Position the stick so that it hides the pin. Glue small bits of moss onto the stick and the mushrooms.

13. Flowers, leaves, or other items, which are sold on single stems or in bunches, can be attached with a wood stick. Cut the stem about 2¹/₂" from the flower head. Wrap the stick's wire tightly around the flower stem.

14. Cut off any excess wire.

15. These flowers are placed next to another mushroom on the wreath. Using odd numbers of various elements is a rule of good design.

16. Cut a length of small-leaved ivy vine and use "U" pins to incorporate it into the wreath. Once all of the main elements are placed and adorned with moss, add smaller items such as pods and pinecones.

17. The spring woodland landscape does not include showy flowers, but if you like, a few small dried and preserved blooms may be added. These were pulled from a bag of potpourri. One of the most difficult things about making a good craft project is knowing when enough is enough. As you're making your wreath, step back to see if the material mix is balanced, but not symmetrical, and full enough to satisfy you.

18. Your moss and mushroom wreath is ready to welcome visitors.

This candelabrum was in pretty bad shape when discovered at a yard sale. It's like new with the addition of fresh moss, pods, dried fern fronds, dried flower heads, and battery-operated candle tapers.

Make a matching clay flower pot and picture frame with moss and dried flowers. Glue moss onto the wrong side of a 4" ceramic tile to make a coaster.

Moss transforms a foam ball into a thing of beauty. Use a low-temperature glue gun or white glue to attach the foam. A dried fern frond adds some dimension.

Garden-Themed clocks

Garden time differs from real time. When tending to the landscape, I feel time whizzes by, and when I'm enjoying the results, it almost stands still. If you need to know the real time, turn to an old-fashioned analog clock that reflects your style. This project takes advantage of the natural beauty of wood. The other examples will get you thinking about how you can transform household and craft items into a one-of-a-kind timepiece.

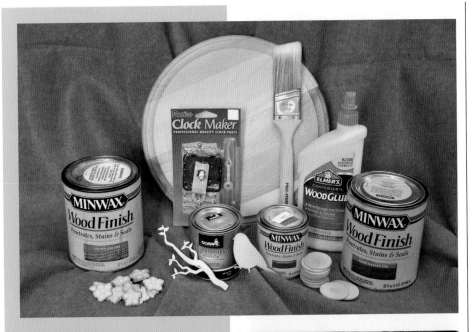

EQUIPMENT

Drill with ¼" bit
Paintbrushes
Latex or rubber gloves

SUPPLIES

Battery-operated clock movement with a 1³/₁₆" shaft length
11" round, unfinished wood clock base
2" unfinished wood disks (12)
12 small unfinished wood flower appliqués
Thin, unfinished wood appliqués— bird and branch, or your choice
Oak stain
Walnut stain
Redwood stain
Dark walnut or black stain
Clear satin polyurethane
Carpenter's glue
Clean-up rags or T-shirt fabric

stain, and then stain the surface, applying stain evenly and in the same direction as the grain.

3. Allow the stain to penetrate for a few minutes, and then wipe off any excess. Pay particular attention to wiping up any drips where the rim meets the work surface. Let the stain dry for four hours. Flip the base over and stain the back.

1. Your round clock base should come pre-sanded and with a predrilled center hole. If it didn't, sand lightly with fine sandpaper (always with the grain). Drill the hole with a ¼" bit. To find the center, trace the disk onto a piece of paper and cut it out. Fold the paper in half and in half again. The center is where the lines cross.

4. Use the light oak color to stain the small flower appliqués, making sure the stain penetrates the depressions. Allow these to dry for four hours. If the stain is not as dark as you would like it to be, apply another coat.

2. Protect your work surface with a tarp or plastic sheeting topped with newspapers or other absorbent material, and protect your hands with latex or rubber gloves. Start by staining the rim of the clock base with light oak

5. Using a fresh rag, apply dark walnut or black stain to the surface and edges of the bird and branch appliqués. Allow these to dry for four hours. Again, apply another coat to darken if needed.

6. Once the clock base is thoroughly dry, use a foam brush or synthetic paintbrush to apply a coat of clear satin polyurethane. As before, coat the rim first and then the surface. Wipe up any drips with the brush. Two thin coats of sealant are preferable to one thick coat. Allow the seal coat to dry thoroughly, flip the clock over, and seal coat the back.

7. Pour a small puddle of carpenter's wood glue in a disposable bowl. Use a fresh foam brush to lightly coat the backs of the wood flower appliqués, center them on the disks, and press lightly.

8. Have a damp paper towel or rag handy to wipe off any glue that squirts out onto the disk. Allow the disks to dry for two hours.

9. Place the disks on a protective surface, and spray them with two coats of matte finish clear acrylic sealant.

10. Trace a clock face template onto tracing paper and cut it out. (See page 181) Find the center by folding the circle in half, and in half again.

11. Poke a nail through the center of the template, and push the nail into the center hole in the clock back.

12. Use several strips of clear tape to secure the template to the clock back. Use a foam brush to apply an even coat of carpenter's glue to the back of a disk. Wipe off any glue from the edge.

13. Line up the center of the hour mark with the center of the first disk. Place the disk on the clock face about $1/2$" from the outer rim. Continue gluing and placing the other eleven disks.

Look at the clock from above to ensure that all the disks are aligned properly. If not, slide them into place. Immediately wipe up any glue that remains, as well as any glue that may have squirted out from the disks.

14. Insert the shaft base through the center hole and place it on your work surface.

15. Determine the placement of the bird and branch appliqués. Apply glue to the backs of these pieces, and press them in place. Have a rag handy to clean up any glue that squirts out onto the clock base.

16. Follow package instructions for placing the clock hands onto the shaft. Typically, you would attach the dial-fixing hex nut, attach the hour hand and press lightly, attach the minute hand, and lightly screw the minute nut in place. (Some kits come with a rubber cushion to be used between the clockworks and the clock base. This may not fit this clock because the bird and branch appliqués take up space.)

17. Install batteries, and your clock is ready to hang in a location where it is sheltered from rain.

The base of this raised garden bed clock is a 12" x 12" square of high density fiberboard (HDF), but ¹/₄" plywood or birch board could also be used. Prime and paint the back of the board. The border uses half-round bamboo sticks from a recycled trellis, but half-round molding that's sealed with polyurethane would also work. The border was attached using ¹/₂" finish nails. Use the clock face template to attach smooth rocks with a generous amount of white PVA glue. The soil was made with simulated soil used for potted plants. You can make your own by combining a cup of very fine bark chips with a couple tablespoons of white glue and ¹/₄ cup of water. Blend to form a paste, and apply to the board with your hands. Wipe off any glue that gets on the rocks. The glue will dry clear.

If the beach is your passion, make a sand and shell clock. Use a 12" x 12" square of high density fiberboard (HDF), ¹/₄" plywood, or birch board.

Prime and paint the back of the board. Attach the shells with white glue, using the clock face template. Run a generous band of glue along the edges and press on heavy jute twine (4-ply, 72# was used here). Wet the twine to make it easier to work with. Coat the entire board with a thick layer of white glue, and sprinkle a generous amount of white craft sand on the surface. Pat the sand down with your hands. Wipe off any glue or sand from the shells.

Flowers and butterflies are a natural choice for a garden clock. Drill a ¹/₄" hole in the center of a 13" plastic charger plate, and apply two coats of spray paint for plastics. Use the instructions for applying decals found on pages 147–49 to apply images at the hour marks and one large image in the center. White images tend to become more translucent when applied to painted surfaces, so they are a great choice to place behind the clock hands. Finish it off with two coats of matte or gloss clear acrylic spray.

Dried & Pressed
flower art

Centuries ago, botanists pressed leaves and flowers to catalog the specimens for identification purposes. More recently, those marvelous crafty women of the Victorian era turned pressing plant materials into an art form. The craft is still alive and well today. Dried and pressed flower clubs and guilds abound around the world. Give your garden flowers life beyond their bloom time using age-old techniques and some new ones, too.

EQUIPMENT

Flower press
Microwave oven
Microwaveable bowls

SUPPLIES

Silica gel
Matte board
Project paper
Picture frame with glass
   (a glass-free frame or shadow box
   may also be used)
Tweezers
Small artist's paintbrush or toothpick
Tweezers
White glue
Dried flower preservative spray

Flowers and Leaves

Many garden flowers can be pressed or dried with good results. Very thin flower petals might become translucent when pressed, but look fine if dried in silica gel. White flowers are not a good choice, as they dry to a tan, cream, or brown color. Some flowers, such as *Hydrangea* and roses, will dry naturally on their stems in a vase of water. Whether you press or dry your flowers depends on your preference and purpose. Pressed flower petals are smooth, while dried ones retain some body and may have a crinkled appearance. Pressed flowers are best for greeting cards and bookmarks. Dried flowers work well for three-dimensional work.

Dried and pressed flowers will retain their color for quite a long time, especially if sprayed with a product that includes UV protection. Leaves press very well and provide a wide range of shades of greens, reds, yellows, and silvers. Artistically, they provide contrast and balance to brightly colored petals. However, they are sure to brown out within a year or less as the chlorophyll breaks down. Colors will last longer if the artwork is kept out of direct sunlight.

Project Papers

Select a project paper that will enhance and not compete with your design. Handmade papers add interest and dimension, but white watercolor or mixed media paper, card stock, and even wallpaper are suitable. Use spray glue to adhere a slightly oversized sheet of paper to a piece of matboard, cardboard or foam core sized to fit your frame. Trim off the excess with scissors or a craft knife.

Flowers, such as this *Rudbeckia*, can be dried whole in silica gel or their petals can be removed and dried individually in a flower press.

Drying Flowers Using a Press

1. You may have tucked a flower in a book as a remembrance of a person or event. Books—especially heavy dictionaries and phone books—produce fine dried material for crafting. Drying time will vary depending on the thickness and water content of the flower and leaves being pressed. Check after two to three weeks. If the petals, leaves, or stems are at all flexible, they are not completely dry. Close the book and check again in another week.

2. Purchased flower presses consist of layers of corrugated cardboard and blotter paper held together by wood panels. Threaded bolts and wing nuts are tightened to evenly distribute pressure.

You can make your own press with two 6" x 6" tiles that are held together with sturdy rubber bands. This homemade press uses construction paper in place of blotting paper. Some crafters prefer to add additional layers of paper between the blotting papers, but it is not necessary. Blotting paper is available at art supply stores.

3. Disassemble the press, but leave the bottom wood panel and the threaded bolts in place. Start filling the press by placing flowers or leaves on the bottom (one or two layers of corrugated cardboard and a layer of blotting paper). Material should not touch, overlap, or hang out over the edge.

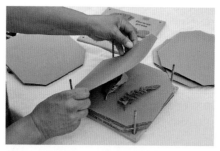

4. As you place a sheet of blotting paper over the material, watch to see that it remains flat.

5. Place a piece of corrugated cardboard over the blotting paper.

6. Arrange more flowers and leaves on the blotting paper; cover it with a sheet of blotting paper and another piece of corrugated cardboard. Continue to load the press until you near the top of the bolts.

7. Top the pile with a piece or two of corrugated cardboard. Place the top wood panel through the bolts and screw on the wing nuts evenly. If you are using a homemade press, hold it closed with four or six heavy duty rubber bands. Check the press in a week or two. If the materials are not dry, close the press and check back a few days later.

8. Store your dried materials in airtight containers until you are ready to use them. If left uncovered, they will absorb moisture in the air.

Drying Flowers with Silica Gel

Silica gel is a non-toxic, naturally occurring mineral that has a high moisture-absorbing capacity. It can be purchased in small bags at most craft stores and online. Most include colored beads which change color when the silica can no longer absorb moisture. The nice thing is that spent silica can be rejuvenated by spreading it out on a baking tray and heating it at 250 degrees for about twenty minutes or until the indicator beads return to their original color.

1. Cut the stem close to the flower head.

2. Place the flower in a container that is half full of silica gel. Slowly pour silica gel over the flower, plus another 1/2" above it.

3. Place a lid on the container. It will take about a week for the flower to dry or you can use a microwave to speed up the process.

4. Place the container in the microwave set at 50 percent power for two minutes. Allow the container to cool for ten minutes or so, then slowly pour out the silica until you can see the flower. Gently pull the flower from the gel.

5. Use an artist's paintbrush, a bamboo skewer, or toothpick to knock off the silica gel beads from the petals.

6. Store your flowers and leaves in an airtight container until you are ready to use them.

Creating Pressed and Dried Flower Art

1. Start by choosing your project paper based on which flowers you will be using. Test the grouping against light and dark backgrounds to see which you prefer.

2. Attach your project paper to matboard, cardboard, or card stock. Cut a sheet of paper to fit the frame, and cut the matboard or cardboard slightly larger. Spray the paper with adhesive, lay the sprayed side down on the backing board, and smooth it out from top to bottom. Cut off the excess backing board.

3. Place the flower petals and leaves in a pleasing arrangement on the project paper.

4. The center parts of a flower (stamens) are often thick and deep and are not usually dried for a two-dimensional design. Check your spice cabinet for suitable substitutes. Here, poppy seeds are sprinkled on a generous circle of white glue. Use a bamboo skewer or toothpick to push seeds onto the glue circle.

5. Some crafters use a toothpick to place only a small amount of glue on the tip of a petal. For superior holding power, use a small artist's brush to lightly apply a thin coat of glue. If the brush drags, thin out the glue with a little water. The glue will dry clear.

6. Pick up the petal with the brush and put it in place. Press the petal down gently with your finger.

7. Continue gluing and placing the elements of your design. The leaves you use need not be from the same flowering plant. Mix and match with what you have to create a design that appeals to you.

8. Layering flowers and leaves will give your project artistic appeal. Here, the stamens were pulled from the flower. A small cluster is placed on its side in a generous puddle of glue.

9. Use a skewer to rearrange the stamens and to ensure that they are well glued. Continue to glue the remaining petals. Finish the flowers by layering more petals on top of the first rows.

10. Overlapping leaves and flowers will result in a natural look. Use two generous dots of glue to hold a stem in place. Use a petal to hide the stem near the flower head.

11. Size the second stem and cut it to fit. Again, use two generous dots of glue to hold the stem in place.

12. Another leaf is needed to fill the gap.

13. A final leaf is cut with scissors and placed to appear as if it is behind the orange flower. Several fallen petals are added as a final touch; one will cover the place where the stem meets the leaf.

14. Allow the glue to dry overnight. Spray the piece with two coats of dried flower preservative spray and let it dry before placing your dried flower art in a nice frame.

This old-fashioned shrub rose and buds were dried in the microwave oven using silica gel and sprayed with flower preservative. Spray glue was used to attach a paper doily to a matboard. The flowers were glued to the backer board using white glue. The rose is showcased in a shadow box frame.

Some dried flower artists use symmetry and repetition to create simple or quite complex designs. Other botanicals, such as these acorns, make for interesting subject matter. Sometimes a simple combination of a few leaves is all that's needed to create a memory of a fun day in the garden or woods.

Think outside the frame. These *Hydrangeas* were left in a vase of water to air dry, and then sprayed with dried flower preservative. The stems were taped with floral tape onto a backing that was already placed in the frame. A generous amount of white glue was placed on the tips of the leaves, which were carefully pressed into place.

Dine
in style

Table Coverings

Setting a nice table starts with the tablecloth. Don't like to sew? Don't have a machine? No worries. You can make your own table coverings with fusible web and fabric glue. Tabletops are always in high demand at garden parties, so this project shows how you can disguise an inexpensive fiberboard occasional table that has a multitude of uses all year long.

EQUIPMENT

Long, sharp scissors

Steam iron

SUPPLIES

Round fiberboard occasional table

2 yards 72" wide polyester felt, color of your choice (for tablecloth)

1¹/₂ yards 45" wide patterned cotton or cotton blend fabric, colors to coordinate with tablecloth (for coverlet)

A ⁵/₈" wide roll of super strength fusible web

Large safety pin

String

Sewing pen with disappearing ink, chalk, or non-permanent felt marker

Selecting Fabrics

Polyester felt comes in a wide range of colors, is easy to cut, washes well, and is cost-effective. Best of all, it is available in 72" widths. (It does tend to pick up lint and pet hair, which can be removed with a lint brush.) Wool felt is also available but is more expensive and tends to shrink quite a bit. Home decorator fabrics come in wide widths, but are prohibitively expensive for the budget-minded.

Burlap comes in a wide range of colors and is inexpensive as well. Widths are usually limited to 45", so it is most suitable for coverlets and placemats.

The world is your oyster when it comes to the many colorful prints, patterns, and solid colors available in cotton and cotton/polyester blends. These are lighter weight fabrics than felt and burlap, making them perfect for coverlets and as appliqués for placemats.

Choosing a Table

The table used in this project is widely available, starting at about $10 in discount stores, home improvement stores, bath and linen stores, and online. The top surface of the one used in this project measures 19¹/₂" and is 25¹/₂" high. To determine the width of your fabric for a skirt that will reach the floor, double the height and add it to the diameter of the top. In this case, the sum is 25¹/₂" times two equals 51", plus 19¹/₂" equals 70¹/₂". This translates into 2 yards of 72" wide felt or other fabric.

Making the Table

1. Knot the end of a 42" length of string to a large safety pin.

2. Fold the fabric in half. To find the center of the fabric, bring together the two edges along the folded side.

3. Insert the safety pin into the two layers of fabric at this center point.

4. Use masking tape to secure the fabric to a hard surface.

5. Wrap the string around the pen several times and grasp the pen and string together.

6. Mark a starting point to draw the cutting line. This point is half the diameter of your cloth. Earlier, we determined that the tablecloth diameter for this table is $70\frac{1}{2}$", so the mark is made at $35\frac{1}{4}$".

7. Place the pen on this mark and rewrap the string if necessary so that your pen is at a 90-degree angle to your work surface. The string should be taut at all times, but not pulling the safety-pinned fabric from the work surface. Slowly draw an arc from the center to one edge of the fabric. Return to the center mark and draw an arc to the other edge of the fabric.

8. Cut slowly and carefully along the line. There is no need to hem felt, so your tablecloth is complete.

Tablecloth Coverlet

Tablecloth coverlets can be made with fabric that is only 45" wide, which gives you a huge range of color and style options. Burlap fabric has an organic, earthy look that coordinates well with animal print and botanical themes. With cotton or cotton blends, you can find almost everything—florals, stripes, dots, paisleys, and more. The cutting technique is the same as for the felt tablecloth.

Measurements for the burlap and the sunflower coverlets shown here were the same. The diameter was $44^5/8$" to make maximum use of the fabric (44" diameter, plus a $^5/8$" hem.) You may have to adjust this downward based on the exact measurements of your fabric. If the fabric was cut unevenly it may be less than 45" in some places.

Fusible web bonds together two layers of fabric and is washable. Package directions for this brand recommend that the iron be set to "wool" and that a damp press cloth be used. If you find that a press cloth tends to get in the way, the hem can be done using the steam feature on the iron instead.

1. Set your iron to the appropriate fabric setting. Start folding under $^5/8$" of fabric toward the back side and press. Continue turning and pressing in short sections until you reach your starting point.

2. Unwind several feet of fusible web. Slip about 4" or 5" under the hem, making sure it is laying flat. Place the iron on this portion of the hem for several seconds, and then lift the iron and check to see that the layers are bonded. Do not slide the iron. Continue in this manner all the way around the coverlet. If the fusible web tape breaks, simply overlap the torn ends slightly and continue.

Mix and match. The golden-brown felt tablecloth is a good base for the off-white burlap and sunflower coverlets.

Tablecloth
weights

A good gust of wind can take your tablecloth and send everything on it tumbling over. Prevent that from happening by clipping a set of tablecloth weights onto your cloth hem. With some inexpensive hardware and the right glue, you can reuse and repurpose silk flowers, charms, key tags, kids' toys, rocks, gems, and other craft odds and ends to match any decorative theme or table setting.

Equipment & Supplies

What you need to do the job will depend on what hardware and decorative materials you are using. The only essentials are 1¹/₄" or 2" non-insulated electrical alligator clips or round craft magnets, and the proper glue to attach your decorative item. If you plan to incorporate beads, shells or other items that will dangle from the clip, you'll need fishing line (monofilament) or florist's wire. In one example, jewelry jump rings were used to connect elements.

About Adhesives

Check your supply of glues to see if one will work for the two materials you are matching up. Weather-resistant glue, super-type glues or clear waterproof silicone sealant will handle most projects. Always read the product package for special instructions. For instance, when using water-resistant white glue (such as Weldbond) to adhere a porous and a nonporous surface, apply the glue to each surface and let it tack up for a couple of minutes. You may also have to hold the alligator clip onto the item until the product tacks up a bit to prevent it from slipping or sliding off some surfaces.

Methods of Attaching Items

1. In most cases, select a size alligator clip that won't overhang the length of your decorative items. There are a couple of exceptions. Use a larger clip when attaching a particularly heavy item that would benefit from additional surface area for gluing. If you want to attach additional items to the clip, extend the bottom of the clip over the edge of the item so that you have access to the pre-made holes.

2. If there is not enough surface area on your item to accommodate the clip, glue a metal washer to the item and the clip to the washer. Select a washer that has the smallest center hole.

3. Decorators use this technique to jazz up lampshades. Glue one craft magnet to your item and place a second magnet behind the cloth on top of the first.

4. Various size jump rings used to make jewelry can be connected to attach elements that hang from the clip.

The butterfly body was glued to the clip with the holes overhanging the edge. Beads were strung on florist's wire, which was inserted into one of the holes and wrapped tight.

Flowers are the perfect choice for the garden-themed table. Plastic beads were threaded on $1/8$" satin ribbons, which were tied to the stem of a silk flower. The stem was inserted into the hole of a metal washer that holds the alligator clip.

A smooth, polished, black stone glued to an alligator clip serves as the weight. The feather was attached to the hole in the clip with a jewelry jump ring.

This large silk sunflower was pulled from its stem and glued to a craft magnet. Another magnet placed behind the cloth holds it in place.

A faux sedum was glued to a metal washer attached to the clip.

Costume jewelry is a good source for decorative elements. The wooden animal and beads were strung on fishing line. Knots were tied at both ends and glued for extra holding power.

Amuse your guests with these crawling salamanders. Prime and paint the salamander and glue a clip to its back.

A simple glass tile was glued directly to an alligator clip.

This key tag charm was glued directly to an alligator clip.

No-Sew
placemats

Add another layer to your outdoor dining table with coordinating placemats. Inspiration abounds in seashore, mountain, animal print, botanical, and desert motifs. Inexpensive burlap serves as a base for painted, appliquéd, and stamped embellishments. Special fabric glue and fusible web allow you to wash or dry clean these no-sew placements for many seasons of use.

EQUIPMENT

Yardstick or tape measure
Long sewing scissors
Straight pins
Steam iron

SUPPLIES
Bright Flower Mats

Yard of burlap in your choice of color
**Cotton or cotton blend fabric print
    that includes a design element
    that coordinates with burlap and
    ribbon**
**6 yards wire-edged or cotton ribbon
    for each mat—2" width was used
    in this project**
**6 yards fusible web tape for each
    mat—2" width**
Sheet of 8" x 10" fusible web
Spray fabric protector

SUPPLIES
Animal Print Mats

**Fabric or acrylic paint—black,
    medium brown, and yellow**
Large rubber stamp
Fabric glue
Spray fabric protector

About Burlap

Burlap is usually sold in 45" widths
and now comes in a wide range of
colors, metallics, and stamped prints.
It is inexpensive and easy to work
with, but it does fray. For this reason
it is best not to prewash burlap before
using it with fabric glue or iron-on
adhesive products. A good coat of
spray fabric protector will allow for
spot cleaning. When a thorough
washing is needed, use cold water
on a delicate cycle, and then press
to finish.

About Paints

Once dry, acrylic craft paints will hold
up and wash as well as those sold as
fabric paints, although the latter may
be more elastic and less susceptible to
cracking. Bottled acrylic (as opposed
to tube paints) can be poured into
plastic containers with pointed tips
for fine line work.

Appliquéd Placemat with Ribbon Border

1. Cut four equal rectangles from 1
yard of burlap. Mark the outline of
the final 18" x 13" placemat size. An
easy way to do this is by making start
and end marks with a pencil in the
four corners.

2. Place the pencil tip on one of the
marks and, using moderate pressure,
drag it across the fabric toward the
end mark. The pencil point will
remain in the groove of the burlap
weave and will give you a perfectly
straight line. Repeat for the remaining
three sides.

3. Use the full fabric rectangle (not
the final placemat lines) to quickly
measure and cut four lengths of ribbon which will form the placemat
border.

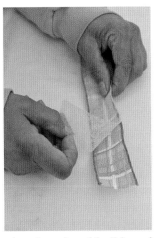

4. Cut four lengths of fusible web from the roll to fit the two long and two short sides of the ribbon border.

5. Place the fusible web on the back side of the ribbon; place a piece of transfer paper over that and press, using high heat and no steam.

6. Be sure that the fusible web remains flat and centered on the ribbon as you go.

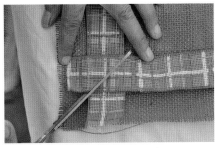

7. Place one long and one short section of ribbon on the placemat border lines. To cut the mitered corners, overlap the two ends of ribbon, making sure they are at 90-degree angles. Cut through both thicknesses of ribbon, from the outside corner where the two ribbons meet to the inside corner.

8. Pin the corners on the diagonal, matching the edges. Repeat for the other three corners. Line up the long edges of the ribbon to the line and pin in place.

9. Fuse the ribbon to the burlap, starting with one corner. Set the iron to high heat and no steam. Press the corner for several seconds then move along the ribbon edge until all ribbon has been fused to the burlap. Remove the pins. Re-press any areas that appear to be loose.

10. Corners made with wire-edged ribbon want to pull up. If necessary, pull up the offending corner and reattach with a generous amount of fabric glue. Press it in place for about thirty seconds.

11. For the center design, a 9" x 12" sheet of iron-on fusible web was placed over a cotton paisley flower print fabric cut slightly larger. Set the iron to the steam setting. (Follow label directions for the product you are using.) Remove the liner paper and press to the wrong side of the fabric. Hold the iron on each section for about ten to fifteen seconds. Overlap as you proceed to fuse the entire piece.

12. Use sharp scissors to cut out the fabric design elements you want to transfer to your placemat.

13. Arrange the pieces the way you want them on the placemat. Peel off the backing paper of your appliqué pieces and place them on the mat where they are to go. Note that some fusible webs enable you to stick your design temporarily to your fabric while arranging and rearranging. The bond is not permanent until you apply steam heat.

14. Once everything is placed where you want it, fuse it to the fabric.

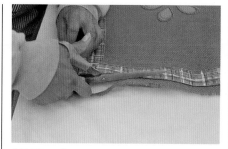

15. Use sharp scissors to cut away the burlap close to the ribbon.

16. Spray the placemat with outdoor silicone fabric protector.

The fabric protector should prevent most spills from seeping into the fabric. When cleaning is needed, wash on gentle cycle, air dry, and press out wrinkles.

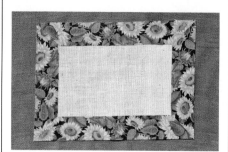

This sunflower placement was made in the same way using cotton ribbon. Ribbon without wire is an easier product to work with, especially for beginners.

Painted Placemats

1. Draw 12" x 17" placemat edges as you did with the ribbon placemats. Be sure to leave $1^{1}/_{2}$" of fabric outside this line on all sides to make the fringe. Draw lines 2" from the outside edge lines to make a wide border all the way around.

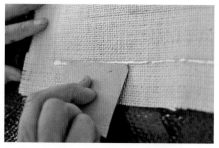

2. To prevent the fabric from fraying into the placemat area, squirt a line of fabric glue or white glue along the outer placemat edge line. Use a piece of cardboard to pull the glue toward the outside edge, forming a narrow glue line. Allow this to dry before continuing.

3. Select a stamp that does not include much detail, which would not transfer well to the rough burlap fabric. Paint the stamp with the color of your choice using fabric or acrylic paint.

4. Position the stamp over the area where you want to make the impression, and press it down firmly and evenly. Carefully lift it straight up.

5. Some crafters like the appearance of a light transfer. If you're not satisfied, simply use a small artist's brush to paint the lighter sections of the transferred image.

6. Use the fine tip nozzle of the fabric paint to form the inside and outside border of the placemat. Because of the rough burlap texture, it's not possible to make a crisp line. The unevenness will only add to the charm of this rustic design.

7. Make puddles of medium brown and yellow on a paper or foam plate. Alternate between two artist's brushes to paint on the medium brown and yellow paint, using long strokes. Blend the two colors as you go. When the brushes become muddy from blending, dip them in water and wipe with a paper towel. Continue painting the entire border, blending well as you go.

8. Draw a 1¹/₂" border around the placemat edge and cut along this line on all sides.

9. Fringe the border by pulling the burlap threads from the fabric.

10. Continue pulling threads until you reach the painted border. The glue line you applied earlier will prevent the fabric from unraveling any farther.

Picture Frame
serving tray

A large serving tray comes in very handy to transport food and drink from the kitchen to the deck or patio. This one uses an open-back picture frame that's seen better days. It can be personalized in so many ways—with photographs, dried and pressed flowers, travel memorabilia or artwork.

EQUIPMENT

Screwdriver
Utility knife
Drill with $1/8$" bit

SUPPLIES

11" x 14" open-back frame
Glass or Plexiglas to fit opening
Matboard to fit opening
High density fiberboard (HDF) or
**   plywood to fit opening**
1" turn buttons with screws (4)—
**   picture framing hardware**
Acrylic paint
Rub 'n Buff
Gold spray paint
Pair of screen door handles or other
**   decorative handles that have only**
**   two screw holes**

1. Wash the frame with mild soap and water to remove debris and oils and allow to dry. Priming the frame will increase paint adhesion and cover any oils or dirt that remains on the frame.

2. For this project burnt umber tube acrylic paint was mixed with a liquid acrylic medium brown to create a nice milk chocolate color. Paint the entire

frame a color that will coordinate with what you plan to frame. If you're not sure what you want to do, select a neutral color. Apply a second coat if necessary, and allow the acrylic paint to dry overnight.

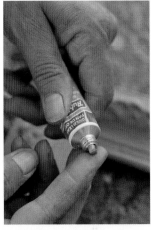

3. If your frame has raised details, highlight them with gold "Rub 'n Buff." The best way to apply this product is to squirt a dot on your finger and swipe across the tops of the raised areas.

4. Use a light touch and don't over apply it. This waxy substance cannot be easily removed. The best strategy if you make a mistake is to complete the frame, and then go back and touch up areas with acrylic paint. Spray the frame with a coat of clear acrylic sealer to make it easy to clean with a damp cloth.

5. If you don't like the finish of your screen door handles, spray paint them and the screws with a matte finish or metallic paint to match your tray.

6. Find the center of the short side of your tray and mark it with a pencil. Measure the distance between the center of your handle holes and divide it by 2. In this case, it is 4 1/8" divided by 2, equals 2 1/16". Use that number (2 1/16") to measure and mark either side of the center mark on the tray.

7. Check to make sure that the handle hole marks line up and make adjustments if necessary.

8. Match your drill bit to the screw shank (the smooth portion without the ridges). In this case, it is 1/8".

9. Drill pilot holes at each mark, about half the depth of your screw, and use a hand screwdriver or drill driver to insert the screws. Repeat the process on the other side.

10. To make an insert, trim a decorative sheet of paper slightly larger than your frame opening. Apply adhesive to the entire sheet. Center the sheet sticky side down over your matboard and press from the center out to prevent wrinkling.

11. Trim the paper to the edge of the matboard.

12. Assemble the tray by placing the glass or Plexiglas in the frame, followed by the decorative sheet and the plywood or high density fiberboard (HDF). If the top board is not flush with the top of the frame edge, add more matte board or cardboard to raise the stack.

13. Mark the center points of all four sides of the frame about ¼" from the inner edge. Drill pilot holes for the fasteners at these marks.

14. Screw the turn button fasteners into the pilot holes.

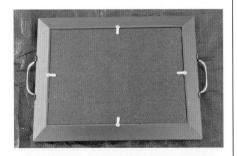

15. You now have a blank canvas on which to craft unique inserts for your new serving tray. It can be easily swapped out by loosening the screws and swiveling the turn buttons.

The decorative paper used in the tutorial serves as a background for a garden of dried and pressed flowers.

Use a favorite art print to fill your frame, or paint your own original work.

Enlarge a garden photograph. Use the close-up feature on your camera to capture a bee, butterfly or flower, or take a shot of a favorite garden bed that includes one of the garden crafts you made.

Make a souvenir tray. Assemble postcards, menus, road maps, photos, and bits of nature from a family excursion. Mount them artfully onto a matboard with a glue stick or white glue. In this example, felt was used as a background to suggest a beach scene. If your items are bulky, instead of glass and HDF you may need to use Plexiglas and matboard, which are more flexible.

Combine media in unique ways. This head shot of one of the family cats peeks out from an assortment of dried and pressed ornamental grasses.

Flower Decal
glassware

Transform plain yard sale and dollar store glassware into useful vases and candleholders with this quick and easy transfer technique. You can use drawings, illustrations, or best of all, photographs from your own garden to make one-of-a-kind table accessories and gifts. These transfers may also be used on tile, wood, and metal, expanding the possibilities to other garden projects.

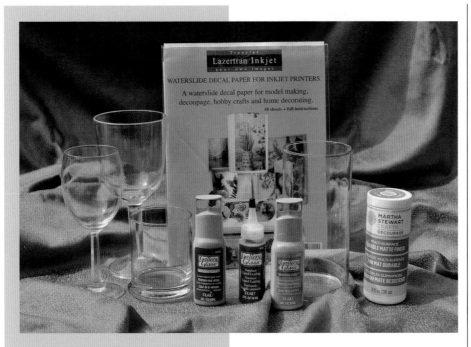

EQUIPMENT

Sharp scissors with short blades
1/2" flat artist's paintbrush
Computer with a graphics program
   (word processing programs will
   also work)

SUPPLIES

Digital photographs or digital
   copyright-free illustrations
Waterslide decal paper to match your
   printer (inkjet or laser)
Rubbing alcohol
Tray of water, sized to accommodate
   largest image
Matte or glossy decoupage medium
   or white glue

About Transfer Paper

Waterslide decal transfer paper is available at art supply and various online stores, but it is hard to locate at most craft stores. Be sure to select the type to match your printer, whether it is an inkjet or laser. Be aware that some transfer papers require a coat of clear acrylic spray to seal the image after it dries. The brand used in the project— Lasertran—does not require that step. Any background areas that are not cut away will appear white, not clear, on your finished piece. (The Lastertran brand includes a solution for that in the instructions for images that will be printed on porous surfaces.)

About Graphic Images

It's hard to top a photograph of flowers from your own garden or drawings that you or your child made for this project. (If you don't have an image scanner, use the services of an office supply copy center.) If you choose to use photographs or illustrations from books or other print materials, be sure to use uncopyrighted work or get permission to use them. If you need directions on placing and

sizing your images to fit a sheet of paper, refer to your software program's "Help" feature. One common error is not sizing the image proportionately. Rather than stretching the top or bottom of your image to fit, resize it so that length and width increase or decrease by the same percentage.

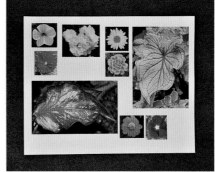

1. Use your computer to arrange your digital images to fit onto an 8.5" x 11" sheet of paper. Print out a test page on regular copy paper to make sure the sizes are correct and the colors are satisfactory. Set the computer print properties according to the waterslide decal paper manufacturer's recommendation. Print the page and allow it to dry for at least thirty minutes.

2. Cut individual images from the full sheet to make them easier to work with. Use sharp scissors to precisely cut out the leaves and flowers. To get crisp edges, keep your scissors stationary while feeding the paper into the blades. Sharply indented areas should be cut in two steps: cut to the point from one outer edge to the center, and then do the same on the other side. The paper should just fall away at the point.

3. Use a paper towel soaked in rubbing alcohol to wipe oils and dust from your glassware and allow it to dry.

4. Place your first image in a shallow tray of lukewarm water for ten to fifteen seconds. Hold edges under water as they start to curl. Flip the image over and allow it to soak for another ten to fifteen seconds, until it is thoroughly saturated.

5. The decal is ready to apply when it slides off the paper backing without resistance.

6. Slip off one edge of the paper backing and apply the decal to the glass. Slowly slide the backing off while laying the decal onto the glass. If the decal wrinkles in any spots, sprinkle a few drops of water onto the area, gently press down on the decal, and pull out the wrinkle.

7. Use a wadded paper towel to gently sop up water drops that remain on the surface of the decal. Continue applying decals in the same manner. Allow the decals to dry thoroughly before applying a protective seal coat.

8. Use a new or very clean ½" synthetic artist's brush to apply decoupage medium. Matte or frosted finish medium was used for this *Caladium* vase. Use long brush strokes from one end to the other, making the medium as smooth as possible. Let the piece dry for two hours, and then apply a second coat. The piece is dishwasher safe on the top rack after it cures for twenty-eight days.

9. *Caladium* leaves, which were the model for this project, are the perfect complement to the frosted *Caladium* vase.

Handling Torn Elements

Wet decals are extremely delicate. If one of your images tears while you are soaking it, place the largest part onto the glass. Wet the area on the glass where the torn piece goes. You should be able to match up the two pieces so the tear is not visible. Very lightly dab the repaired are with a paper towel. If you're not pleased with the result, don't let the decal dry on the glass. Remove the decal right away and replace it later.

You can salvage torn decals by letting them dry on a countertop or foam plate. Cut the dry decals with care. Chances are, most of the decal glue will have washed off, so use decoupage medium or thinned white PVC glue to adhere them to another surface.

Flowers adorn a wine glass (finished with matte medium) and dollar store candle holder (finished with clear gloss medium). The flower touching the rim of the wine glass was cut prior to wetting the decal paper. Beside the wine glass, this votive candle holder was first painted on the inside with green translucent glass paint. Flower decals and two coats of gloss decoupage medium completed the project.

Waterslide decals may be used on a wide range of crafty projects. Birds or flowers would make a great theme to decorate 4" ceramic tiles for a grouted serving tray. An owl is featured on a 12" floor tile. A masonry bit was used to make two $1/4$" holes to accommodate a leather hanging strap. For items that will be heavily used, apply several coats of gel decoupage medium. Wall art just needs an application of clear acrylic spray.

Painted
place settings

If you've coordinated the tablecloth, placemats, and candleholders, creating matching glassware is the logical next step. Designs from the dainty to the dramatic are possible with the wide range of glass paint colors and finishes available. Dollar store and discount store shelves are full of inexpensive glass plates, drinking glasses, serving bowls, candle holders and vases. By using stencils and paper patterns, you need not be adept at freehand painting to produce good results. Can't use glass by the pool? No problem. Multi-surface acrylics can be used on plastic.

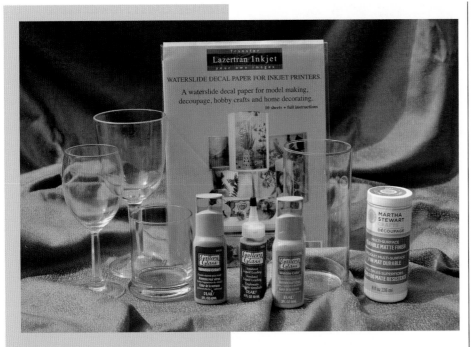

EQUIPMENT

Craft knife and self-healing mat for stenciling

Artist's brushes, sponge roller, or palette knife for painting, depending on the technique used.

SUPPLIES

Glassware—plates, cups, vases, bowls

Rubbing alcohol

Paper towels

Contact paper if making stencils

Black stained glass liquid leading paint

Assorted colors of stained glass paints

About Glass Paint

Glass is a difficult substance to paint on because it has no "tooth" for the paint to stick to. Don't expect to get the smooth and even finish of factory painted glassware that is sold in stores. That said, things that are handmade should look handmade, and have a charm and value that a purchased piece could never have.

Glass paints come in a wide range of colors and can be mixed to make additional colors and hues. There are also a number of finishes from which to choose, including high gloss, satin, translucent, and frosted. Regular acrylic paints can also be used to paint on glass; however, the specialty glass paints advertise a harder finish. Although manufacturers say that items can be machine washed, hand-washing is a safer choice. Curing takes about a month. Instructions for a quick dry curing process using the oven are included with the paint product packaging.

Stained glass paint is not a substitute for the real thing, but produces a similar bright, translucent look. The most important thing to know about these paints before you begin is that some of the colors are dramatically different once they dry. Experimentation is a must if you want to color match. These paints are sold in bottles with needle nose tips, and in sampler packs of small pods, which is a nice option for a newcomer to the craft. Pod paints are scooped out with a small spoon that is provided. The other end of the spoon is used to spread the paint.

Stained Glass Techniques

1. Wipe a clean glass with a rubbing alcohol-soaked paper towel or rag to remove dust and oils.

2. Animal prints are popular gift wrap and fabric themes and can be used as patterns to replicate the fur of cheetahs, leopards, giraffes, and zebras. If you have a scrap of fabric or paper with an animal print, place a small square against the inside of the glass as a pattern. This technique also works with floral, paisley and other all-over designs.

3. Use black glass paint or stained glass liquid leading to apply the design. Using an applicator bottle can be tricky at first, so make a practice line or two on a paper plate before you paint on the glass. Occasionally, you may need to shake the bottle over the paper plate to force the paint into the applicator tip. Squeeze the bottle so that a bead of paint is at the tip. Place the tip on the glass and squeeze the bottle gently to get the paint flowing. Make the line in one smooth motion. Wipe off any mistakes right away with a damp paper towel or cotton swab.

4. If you don't have a pattern, place a plain white paper in the glass and create your own pelt design. The cheetah pelt is composed of irregular ovals, "U" and comma shapes. Orient them in different directions for a realistic effect. Do not paint the top $^1/_2$" to $^3/_4$" of the drinking glass. Allow the paint to dry overnight. This paint takes a very long time to cure. You can check for tackiness by lightly touching one of the lines with the knuckle of one finger. As long as the paint is firm and not wet, you can proceed with the next step.

5. Stained glass paint will change color as it dries. This harvest yellow color dried to a much lighter yellow. A brown or tan would also serve as good background colors. Glass paint that is included in sampler packs comes in small pods and is applied with a small spoon that is provided. Spoon the background color onto the glass between and around the black paint. The paint is easily distributed with the tip of the spoon. A craft stick can be substituted as an applicator. Another way to apply the background color is with an applicator bottle. Squirt a small amount of paint between the black outlines and spread it out with a craft stick or toothpick. When painting the rim, it is not necessary to make a perfectly straight line. Again, keep the paint about $^1/_2$" down from the rim. To make a matching plate, tape the pattern to the top of the plate and paint the underside in the same manner.

Stained Glass Flower Plate

1. The same technique can be used for other designs. Print out a larger daisy-like flower slightly smaller than your plate. Cut it out and tape it to the top of the plate.

2. Clean the back of the plate with rubbing alcohol.

3. Use the black liner paint in an applicator bottle to outline the center of the flower, and then outline each petal. Let the plate dry for several days.

4. These petals must be painted with a needle nose tip bottle. Squirt a thin line of red stained glass paint down the center of each petal. Surround the red with yellow stained glass paint, being careful not to blend the two colors. This paint will shrink slightly as it dries, so be sure the paint touches all black outlines. Pop any air bubbles with a toothpick or pencil point.

5. Spoon or squirt paint into the center of the flower. Use the back of a spoon or a craft stick to spread the paint evenly over the circle. Paint the rim of the plate in the same way with blue stained glass paint.

6. Allow your plate to air dry and fully cure for about three weeks before using it.

How to Use Stencils

Stencils made for glass painting work well. The adhesive back makes them easy to apply and prevents paint from flowing underneath. They are strong enough to be used multiple times. Often, though, the outside margins are too narrow, so clean up around the stencil edge is almost always necessary. Regardless of how you apply the paint, remove the stencil right away while the paint is wet. Paint that has dried will pull off with the stencil. Rinse your stencil right after using it, taking care not to tear it.

1. Position the stencil on the plate and press down all edges. Typically, with palette knife work, you would run a band of paint on one edge and push it across the stencil to the other side. This proves to be very difficult on glass. If you don't have enough paint to begin with, there will be unpainted sections where you end up. For best results, cover the entire stencil with an excess of paint. Hold the knife ever so slightly above the stencil and pass it from one side to the other. Unused paint can be replaced in the bottle for reuse. With practice, you will get good results with less paint.

2. Remove the stencil and rinse if off right away. Clean up any paint that fell outside the stencil with a damp paper towel. Each of the four colors in this stencil is allowed to dry before another color is applied.

Sponge Roller Application

1. Place a puddle of paint on a paper plate. Roll the sponge applicator back and forth until it has picked up plenty of paint. Roll it over the stencil several times until the glass is coated with paint. The paint will have a bubbly appearance.

2. Remove and rinse the stencil right away. Clean off any paint outside of the stencil area with a damp paper towel.

Making Your Own Stencil with Brush Application

1. Simple shapes are the easiest stencils to make and use, but complicated patterns such as monogram letters are possible with practice. Trace or draw a flower petal on paper and cut it out. Tape a section of clear contact paper to a self-healing mat or other cutting surface. Trace the paper petal onto a section of clear contact paper.

2. Use a craft knife to carefully cut on the traced lines. Allow a generous border when you trim the stencil. Separate the two layers of the contact paper. Apply the petal stencil to the glass. Press down all edges of the stencil so that no paint will seep underneath.

3. Brush strokes are inevitable when painting on glass, regardless of whether you use all-surface, enamel, or straight acrylic paints. To minimize brush strokes, use a soft synthetic brush and apply a thick layer of paint. Do not touch the brush to the surface of the glass—just skim the surface of the paint. Another technique that may work to minimize brush strokes is to use the side of the brush to lightly push the surface of the paint. To paint all petals at the same time, overlap the stencil borders as you place them, and remove them in reverse order after painting. Otherwise, you need to allow each petal to dry before proceeding to the next.

4. Remove the stencil right away and clean up any paint that fell outside of the stencil with a damp paper towel.

Sponge Application

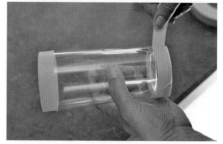

1. Sponging is a quick and easy method of applying paint to stenciled areas or an entire piece. Start by washing the glass and wiping it with rubbing alcohol. Mask the top rim $1/2$" to $3/4$" with tape. Masking the bottom of the glass is optional.

2. Place two or three coordinating colors of gloss enamel or all-surface paint on a paper plate. Pick up one of the colors with the corner of a well wrung-out foam sponge and pounce it on the glass. Pick up more paint as needed and turn the sponge in different directions as you go. Flip the sponge to a fresh corner, dip it in the second color of paint and pounce that on. Overlap the edges slightly where it meets the first color. Add a third highlight color if desired. Continue until the entire glass is sponged.

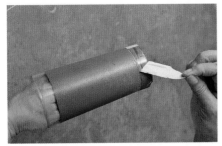

3. Remove the tape before the paint is dry.

4. Allow the glass to fully cure for a month before using it. Check your product packaging for quick-dry instructions if you want to use your piece right away.

Create a tequila sunrise by sponging orange, red, and yellow in bands of varying widths. Use the long side of the sponge to blend the edges between colors.

Paint pens are available in dozens of colors and produce a crisp, opaque line. They are great for monogramming, drawing freehand shapes, and outlining graphic elements.

Pick up a pencil with an unused eraser and just dip and dot. This design makes good use of a sampler pack of high gloss enamels. Have a paper towel handy to wipe off the eraser between colors and use a damp paper towel to wipe off any goofs from the glass as you are painting.

Attract
the birds, bees
& butterflies

Hanging Tray
bird feeder

Tray feeders attract a wide variety of birds, including cardinals, chickadees, doves, grosbeaks, titmice, and native sparrows. The main component of this hanging version is a repurposed open-back art frame that can be purchased for a song at yard sales and thrift stores. It's easily removed for cleaning and can be decorated to suit your style.

2. Measure the length and width of the frame opening, including the lipped edges. Add $1/2$" to the length and width. For this frame, the screening dimensions would be 9" x 11".

3. Cut the screen. At one corner of the screen, measure 9" from the edge in several places and draw a line. From the other edge, mark 11" in and draw a line that intersects the other line. Cut out the screen on the lines.

4. Center the screen on the back of the frame. Staple the screen to the frame starting in the center of one side, as close to the frame edge as possible. Pull the screen taut and place another staple on the opposite side. On one of the unstapled sides, draw the screen tightly and place a staple in the center. Do the same on the opposite side.

EQUIPMENT

Heavy duty stapler with $1/4$" staples
Two sets of pliers
Hand wood saw
Scissors
Tack hammer
Wire cutters
$1/2$" finish nails
Drill with $1/16$" bit
Pencil
Yardstick

SUPPLIES

Open-backed frame to fit an 8" x 10" picture (outside dimensions may vary)
Vinyl window screening material ($1/2$" larger than width and length of frame opening)
2 yards of #16 jack chain or similar decorative chain rated to support 10 pounds
$1/4$" flat screen molding or $1/4$" square dowel to fit frame opening (two times width plus two times length)
Carpenter's outdoor wood glue
$1/2$" eye hooks (4)
$1/2$" closed "S" hook
Heavy 2" open "S" hook
40 upholstery tacks or thumbtacks

1. Clean the frame with mild soap and water and allow it to dry. Use medium grit sandpaper to sand off any splintered wood. Priming a used frame is a good idea even if you plan to use a deck stain or paint that does not require primer. This will seal in any oil or dirt residue and provide maximum paint adhesion. Paint both sides of the frame the color of your choice. Prime and paint the $1/4$" screen molding or square dowel as well.

5. Draw one corner of the screen taut and staple it to the frame on either side of the center staples. Repeat for the other three corners. Trim off the excess screening material in the corners with scissors.

6. Transfer the inside frame measurement—in this case 10"—to a length of screen molding. Place the molding on a vise or other support and cut two lengths using a hand saw.

7. Fit the two lengths along the inside edges. Now measure between the two to get the measurement for the short sides of the screen molding. In this project, the width is 6½".

8. The two short lengths should fit snugly. Remove the four sections of molding.

9. Run a bead of outdoor carpenter's wood glue along the lip, replace the four sections of molding, and press in place. Clean up any wood glue that may have squirted out.

10. Tack ½" finish nails at each corner and the center of all four lengths of molding.

11. Flip the frame over and use a drill with a ¹⁄₁₆" bit to create ¼" deep pilot holes at each corner for the screw eye hooks. Screw each hook into the pilot hole until the eye meets the wood.

12. Cut four 18" lengths of chain. Be sure each length has the same number of links. Use one set of pliers to hold the last link of chain and the other to twist apart the link. Attach the open link to the screw eye and close the link. Repeat for the other three lengths of chain.

13. Use the two-plier technique to open the one end of the closed "S" hook. Slip the ends of all four chains onto the "S" hook.

14. Make sure the feeder hangs straight before closing the end of the "S" hook.

15. Add a decorative touch to your tray feeder by evenly spacing upholstery tacks along the edge.

16. Your tray feeder is ready for action. This one is hung from a shepherd's hook that is attached to a deck rail with bungee cords. Cardinals, snow birds and titmice are just some of the birds in the Northeast that enjoy this hanging feeder.

Male Cardinal.

Titmouse.

For this more fanciful version, apply two coats of bright blue acrylic paint, followed by clear acrylic sealer spray. Plastic gems were glued on using waterproof white glue. (Weldbond was used for this project.)

Woodland
suet feeder

Suet is a high-energy food source that is especially important when food supplies are low and when birds are raising their young. A combination of animal fat, seeds, nuts, and fruits, suet is sold in blocks to fit in metal cages. These cages swing wildly when birds land, making them struggle to perch and feed. The birds love the stability this feeder provides, and you will enjoy seeing more birds and more species of them at your feeding station.

2. Find and mark the center point of one of the short sides. Use a $^1/_8$" drill bit to make a pilot hole $^1/_2$" deep at the center mark.

3. If you don't have one large piece of bark, you can piece together two or three lengths. To prepare the bark, use a hand saw to make the top and bottom edges straight. A slight over-hang on the bottom is preferable to cutting the bark too short.

4. Squeeze a generous amount of outdoor wood glue onto the back of the bark piece, and use a foam brush to distribute the glue evenly over the bark.

EQUIPMENT

Hand saw
Ruler or tape measure
Tack hammer
Drill with $^1/_8$" bit
4 wood clamps
Pliers

SUPPLIES

8" x 12" plywood or pine panel, $^1/_2$"
  thick*
Bark with deep indentations to cover
  the panel
Deck stain or outdoor paint
Paintbrush
Purchased suet cage
Large eye bolt with threaded end
$^1/_2$" wire staples
2" finish nails
Carpenter's wood glue
Foam brush
***If using pine, attach a cap board**
  made of $^1/_2$" wide screen molding
  with glue and finish nails. This will
  help prevent the pine board from
  warping.

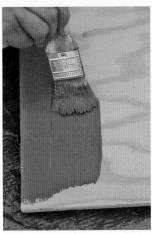

1. Paint the board to protect it from moisture. A primer coat is not needed with this deck paint, but check your product for guidance.

5. Place the board on the wet glue, with the sides centered and the top even with the bark edge.

6. Place clamps evenly around the board. Use a tack hammer to pound eight 2" finish nails randomly around the board. Nail them through the bark and into the board, stopping when the head of the finish nail is flush with the bark. Allow the glue to dry overnight before proceeding. If you wish to make your feeder double sided, repeat the process of attaching the bark from Steps 6 through 8.

7. Remove the clamps. Roughly center the suet cage in all directions, with the top facing the side with the pilot hole drilled in Step 2. Open the cage, place a cable staple over a cage wire

Commercial suet cakes are convenient and inexpensive. Some are advertised as "no melt" for summer or warm climate feeding. You can save money by making your own suet; recipes can be found on the Internet. Make individual cakes in sandwich-sized plastic containers or make a log in a meatloaf pan and cut 1" slices.

near one of the corners, and hammer it in. You may have to angle the staple to accommodate the irregularities in the bark. Place a cable staple near each remaining corner. These are nearly invisible when installed, so careful placement is not essential.

8. Screw the eye hook into the pilot hole. You may need to use pliers to twist the hook so the eye meets the wood.

9. Add an "S" hook, place a suet cake into the cage, and get ready to enjoy the show.

Piecing Narrow Bark Strips

1. If you don't have one single bark piece that's large enough to cover your board, use two or three smaller ones. Glue the back and position them together as best as you can. Clamp each piece and use three or four finish nails per segment. (If the clamps won't reach to the center, use books or another heavy weight. Allow the glue to dry overnight before nailing.)

2. Cover any gaps where wood shows through by gluing bark pieces over them. Put at least one finish nail in each segment. If a piece of bark hangs over the edge, gently pound the bark next to the edge to get a straight break.

These are just some of the birds in the northeast U.S. that enjoy this double-sided bark suet feeder: a Titmouse (top), Black Capped Chickadee (bottom), and a Wren (back).

Wild Bird
nesting box

A garden is not complete without the sight and sound of songbirds. One of the greatest pleasures of a spring day is watching the young ones being fed, growing, and leaving the nest for the first time. This simple wood nesting box will provide comfy quarters for several bird species and hours of fun for gardeners.

EQUIPMENT

Hand saw or circular
    saw
Hammer
Drill Driver with ¹/₈"
    and ¹/₄" bits and a
    1¹/₄" paddle
    (butterfly) bit or a
    1¹/₄" forstner bit
Awl or pencil
Measuring tape and
    carpenter's square

SUPPLIES

1" x 6" x 4' pine
    board (Note that board width is
    actually only 5¹/₂".)
1¹/₂" 4D galvanized common nails
8D common nail
Wood stain
Spar varnish

About Birdhouses

Different species of birds have different needs and wants in their nesting boxes. Box size, entrance hole size and placement, ventilation, and clean-out capability are all important aspects of box construction. The Audubon Society, reputable bird organizations, state university extension agencies, and state wildlife departments are all good sources of information.

This box is designed to fill the needs of House Wrens, Black Capped Chickadees, White Breasted Nuthatches, Prothonotary Warblers and Tufted Titmice. This box can be made with one 1" x 6" x 4' board. Treated lumber should not be used, nor should paints, stains, or seal coats be applied to the inside of the box. The outside can be painted or stained.

1. Carefully measure and use a carpenter's square to draw cutting lines on the 1" x 6" x 4' board at these lengths: three boards measuring 8" for the sides and front; one board measuring 8¹/₄" for the roof; one board measuring 11" for the back; and one board measuring 5¹/₂" for the floor. Select one of the 8" boards for the front. To place the entrance hole, measure 1⁵/₈" from the top of the board and make a mark.

2. Use a carpenter's square to draw a straight line across the board on the mark.

3. Find the center of the board and make a cross mark on the line. To find the center, measure the width and divide that number in half. This is the center of the entrance hole. Drill a pilot hole on the center mark using a ¹/₈" drill bit.

4. Place the front panel on a piece of scrap wood. Here, a forstner bit attached to a drill press is used to drill the 1¹/₄" entrance hole into the front panel. You can also use a 1¹/₄" spade (butterfly) bit on a handheld drill. Be sure to keep the drill in a vertical position and drill slowly with even pressure. Clamp the board securely in place if you use the spade bit. Here's a tip for drilling a perfectly smooth hole: Rather than drilling the hole in one pass, drill the hole only three-quarters through the board. Flip it over and finish drilling the hole at the center mark.

Carpenter's Tip for Finding the Center of a 1" x 6" Board

Our project board actually measures $3/4$" x $5^5/8$". If you measure $2^3/4$" from each edge to the center, you'll have two closely-spaced marks. The center is in between these two lines.

5. Make ventilation holes on side panels. On each 8" side panel, mark 1" from each side and $1^1/2$" from the top. Drill $1/4$" holes at each mark on both boards.

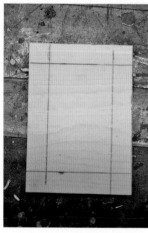

6. Make ventilation holes on the floor. Make a line $3/4$" from the edge on all four sides of the 4" x $5^1/2$" floor panel.

7. Using a $1/4$" drill bit, make four holes where the lines intersect.

8. Hammer four 2" finish nails partway into the front panel. The nails should be placed $3/8$" in from the long edge and evenly spaced along the length of the board. Place the front panel on top of two sides. Line up the front panel evenly to one side panel. (The other side panel is just being used as support.) Hammer the four finish nails through the front panel into the side panel.

9. Hammer three 2" finish nails partway into the roof. The nails should be $3/8$" from the long edge. Space the nails evenly throughout the 8" from the back edge going 8" toward the front. (You do not want to nail into the overhang.)

10. Hammer the 2" finish nails through the roof into the side panel.

11. Use a carpenter's square to mark a line where the roof overhangs the front panel. Attach the roof to the front panel with three 2" finish nails. Place one in the center and the other two on the outer edges, 1" from each edge.

12. Place the unattached side panel on your work surface and place the box on top of it. Fit the floor so that it is flush with the two side and front panels. Attach the side to the floor with three 2" finish nails. Place them ³/₈" in from the edge. Place one in the center and the other two 1" from each outside edge.

13. Use two 2" finish nails to attach the floor to the front panel. These should be placed ³/₈" in from the outside edge. Select any two locations where they will not penetrate the drainage holes.

14. Draw a line on the back panel 2¹/₂" in from the edge of the roof.

15. Transfer the location of the line to the edges on each side of the back panel.

16. Place the box on the work surface with the roof overhanging the edge. Align the edge marks you just made to the center of the roof. Note that the bottom of the back panel will extend below the floor of the box. Use three 2" finish nails to attach the back panel to the roof. Starting at the center, hammer a nail through the back panel into the roof. Be sure the back panel is aligned to the roof properly, and then place the other nails on either side of the center, 1" from each edge.

17. Use three 2" finish nails to attach the back panel to the side. These should be placed ³/₈" from the outside edge and 1" in from the outer edge. Be careful not to hammer a nail through the ventilation hole.

18. Use a carpenter's square to make a nail line on the back panel as shown. This line position should be made in the center of the floor board, which is ³/₈" from the edge of the floor panel.

19. Secure the back panel to the floor with two 2" finish nails.

20. The final side needs to pivot so that the box can be opened for cleaning.

21. To provide a space for the panel to pivot, leave about a $1/8$" gap at the top.

22. Make marks on the front and back boards $5/8$" from the top and $3/8$" from the side.

23. Hammer in a 4D galvanized common nail through the front panel into the side panel at the mark. Repeat the process on the back board. This nail allows for the side to pivot open and closed so that you can clean out the box annually.

24. The final construction step is to secure the side panel with a removable nail. This nail should be placed on the right side. Drill a pilot hole using a $1/8$" drill bit 1" from the bottom and $3/8$" from the side. Hold the side closed when drilling this hole. Cut off one #8D common nail so that it is $1^1/4$" long. Tap it gently through the front and into the side to hold the side closed. You should be able to remove this nail by hand.

25. Use a synthetic brush to apply a coat of wood stain to the outside only. Use a paper towel or rag to wipe off excess stain. Allow the stain to dry and air out for several weeks to allow the stain fumes to evaporate before hanging it for use. Use aluminum nails to firmly attach your nesting box to a tree or post.

Solitary Bee
nesting box

Bees are an essential part of our ecosystem and ensure our survival by pollinating our food crops. You can help support native bee populations by installing a nesting box for wood- and cavity-nesting bees. These bees are non-territorial and non-aggressive, so they rarely sting people. Their habitat has declined, and they are more important than ever given the tremendous loss of the honey bee due to colony collapse disorder. This easy-to-make box will help them reproduce. They will return the favor by pollinating your flowers and vegetables.

EQUIPMENT

Circular saw or hand saw
Drill or driver
Drill bits—$^1/8$", $^3/16$", $^1/4$", $^5/16$", $^3/8$", $^1/4$"
Hammer
2" (#6) finish nails
Carpenter's triangle, speed square, or ruler
Pencil

SUPPLIES

Untreated wood*
2" x 6" boards cut to 7$^1/2$" length (5)
1" x 8" board cut to 7$^1/2$" length
1" x 4" board cut to 12" length
$^3/4$" x $^3/4$" board cut to 7$^1/2$" length
2$^1/2$" deck screws
2" finish nails
***Cedar repels insects, so it is not a suitable choice.**

This nesting box is well suited for mason, sweat, polyester, squash, leaf-cutter, alkali, carpenter, and digger bees. Rather than forming hives, the female solitary bee makes a nest for her eggs in dead wood, rock crevices or holes in bare soil. Their habitat is reduced when gardens are cleaned up in the fall after the eggs are laid. Development has further threatened them by removing habitat and food sources.

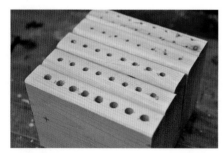

1. This box features nesting cavities in various sizes to suit the needs of different species of solitary bees. The female bee will enter a hole, lay eggs, and then seal it up with a mixture of

saliva and mud (leafcutter bees use leaves) to protect the eggs. Only one row of holes is drilled in the bottom four blocks. Two rows are drilled in the top block.

2. Make a lengthwise line in the center of four of the blocks. Make eight marks for the holes along the line, spaced $^3/4$" apart and 1$^1/4$" from each edge. If you plan to make more than one of these boxes, it makes sense to create a pattern such as this. Place the pattern over the edge of each block and make an indentation by inserting an awl or other sharp tool into the center of each hole.

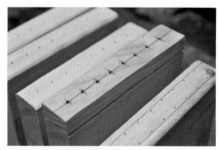

3. Two rows of eight holes are made in only one of these blocks. Make guidelines that are $^3/4$" apart and $^3/8$" from the top and bottom edge. Mark hole placement along the line, spacing them $^3/4$" apart and starting 1$^1/4$" from each edge.

4. Drill eight holes of the same size into each block. Be careful not to angle the drill bit. Drill eight $^3/8$" holes in one block; eight $^5/16$" holes in another block; and eight $^1/4$" holes in the third block. All holes should be 5" deep.

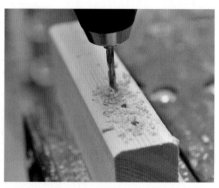

5. Drill eight $^3/16$" holes into block four. Drill sixteen $^1/8$" holes into block five. All holes in these blocks should be 3" deep.

6. Attach block one ($^3/8$" holes) to the bottom of block two ($^5/16$" holes) with two 1$^3/4$" deck screws. Place the screws in the right and left corners, being careful not to screw into the nesting holes. Attach block three ($^1/4$" holes) to block four in the same way.

7. Attach block four ($^3/_{16}$" holes) to block three as the others. Attach the last block, five, (two rows of $^1/_8$" holes) to block four in the same way.

8. Place the blocks upside down on your work surface. Use a carpenter's triangle to make a guideline for the mounting board that is 1$^3/_4$" from each edge.

9. Place the 12" long mounting board along the guidelines so that 5" extends above the block and 1$^1/_2$" extends below. Use 1$^3/_4$" deck screws to attach the mounting board to the

nesting box. Place one screw through the mounting board into the bottom block of the nesting box, about 1" from the edge. Place a second screw diagonally from the first through the mounting board and into the top block of the nesting box, about 1" from the edge. Place a third screw through the mounting board into the center of the nesting box.

10. Align the edges of the $^3/_4$" x $^3/_4$" x 7$^1/_2$" roof support to the nesting box and press it against the mounting board. Attach it by nailing a 2" (#6) finish nail on either side, about 1$^1/_2$" from each edge.

11. Place the roof onto the roof support, aligning each side, and press it against the mounting board. Attach the roof with three 2" (#6) finish nails hammered through the roof into the roof support, in the center and about

1" in from each side. Repeat on the front side, using three 2" finish nails to attach the roof to the top 2" x 6" block, 1$^1/_2$" in from the overhang edge. Drill one $^1/_4$" hole in the centers of both the top and bottom of the mounting board for hanging the nesting box.

12. Bees are particularly sensitive to pollutants. Do not paint the nesting box or use any protective finish inside or out. Before you hang the box, clean out any holes that contain sawdust or splintered wood. Mount the box securely, using drywall screws or galvanized nails, about 4' to 6' above ground, preferably under an overhang. Ideally, the box should be placed so that it gets morning sun and is near flowering plants. Note that some bees may seal the hole deeper into the chamber, rather than at the end. If bees do not start using the box after a few weeks, try moving it to a different location.

Butterfly shelter

One of the best things you can do to attract and support butterflies is to plant plenty of the native flowers they like. To brighten your day and jazz up your garden, make one of these eye-catching butterfly houses. The truth is that experts doubt that butterflies actually use these houses to sleep or escape bad weather. So consider this project a fine way to advertise your love for butterflies and mark their special garden area.

EQUIPMENT

Circular saw or hand wood saw
Hammer
Protractor
Drill with a ½" bit
Screwdriver
Jigsaw
Nail set or awl

SUPPLIES

1" x 8" x 8' pine board
1" x 10" x 4' pine board
2" finish nails
1¼" finish nails
Outdoor enamel paint
Paintbrush
Purchased wood appliqués
Outdoor carpenter's glue
Piece of bark about 4" wide x 23" long (strip may be pieced)
¾" galvanized threaded pipe, 36" long
¾" pipe flange
½" long galvanized countersink head wood screws (4)

1. Lay out the following board dimensions and mark cutting lines directly on the lumber. Wear safety glasses and saw the boards with either a circular or a hand saw.

From the 1" x 8" x 8' board cut:
    Two boards 30" long for the sides
    One board 30" long by 5⅝" for the back
    One board 5¾" x 5⅝" for the bottom
    Note the finished size of a 1" x 8" board is actually only ¾" x 7¼" to 7½".

From the 1" x 10" x 4' board cut:
    One board 28" x 5⅝" for the front
    One board 8⅝" for the roof
    One board 5¾" x 5½" for the roof block
    One board 2" x 25" for the inside mounting strip
    Note the finished size of a 1" x 10" board is actually ¾" x 9¼" to 9½".

2. Use a protractor to draw a 33-degree angle on one end of the 8" x 30" side panel. If you don't have a protractor, place a mark at 28" and draw a straight line from the mark to the opposite corner of the board. Repeat with the other 30" side panel.

3. Cut the angles along the lines with either a circular or hand saw.

4. Use a jigsaw or hand saw to cut off the two corners of one narrow side of the roof.

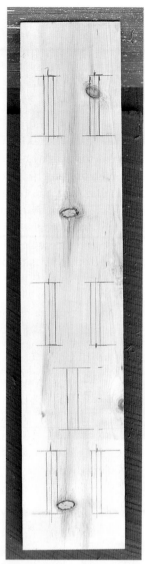

6. Use two blocks to raise the front panel off of the work bench. Clamp the panel to the workbench.

7. Use a $1/2$" drill bit to make holes at both ends of each slot. Drill all fourteen holes in the same manner.

5. Mark the butterfly entrance slots on the 28" by $5^5/8$" front panel. The slots measure $1/2$" wide x $3^1/4$" long. The top two slots begin 4" from the top and $2^1/4$" on center from each edge. The two bottom slots begin 3" from the bottom and $2^1/4$" on center from each edge. The center slot begins 8" from the bottom and is centered. The remaining two bottom slots begin 13" from the bottom and are $2^1/4$" on center from each end.

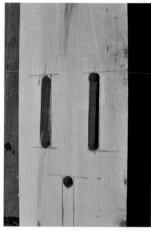

8. Place the jigsaw blade in one of the drilled holes and cut one side of the slot along the line to the second hole. Pull the blade out, replace the blade in the initial hole and cut along the other line to the hole. The wood slot piece should fall out. Repeat the process for the remaining slots.

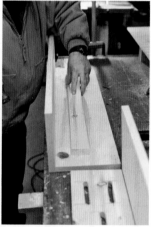

9. Lay the slotted front panel on the work bench. Stand up the two sides with the long edge facing up. Place the back onto the two side edges and align them to the sides. Nail six 2" finish nails through the back panel into the side panel, $3/8$" from the edge and about 4" apart. Just in case butterflies discover this box, the design includes a bark strip for them to grab onto. In nature, butterflies will seek out trees with heavily indented bark to park for the night. Set aside the front and unattached side panels. Center the bark mounting strip on the side panel. Nail it on with four $1^1/4$" finish nails spaced about 4" apart.

10. Use a jigsaw or hand saw to cut the bark to fit the width and length of the nailing strip. Several lengths of bark can be pieced together.

11. Use 2" finish nails to secure the bark to the strip.

12. Replace the side panel and front panel, and align the edges. Attach the back panel to the side panel using 2" finish nails as you did in step 9.

13. Flip the box on its side. Insert the floor panel and align the edges. Clamp the pieces together to keep the panels flush while nailing. Fasten the side to the floor with three 2" finish nails. Don't nail into the overhang. Attach the other side and the back to the floor in the same manner.

14. Flip the box on its back and slide the front panel in the end with two slots at the top. Align the top and bottom edges. Nail three 2" finish nails through the front panel into the floor.

15. Place the box on the floor with the angled edges facing up. Align the roof evenly and use 2" finish nails to secure it on both sides and along the back. Do not place nails along the front edge.

16. Use a straight edge to determine the center of the floor by making an "X" from one corner of the floor panel to the other corner.

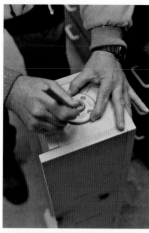

17. Center the pipe flange on the floor panel and make a pencil mark in each of the holes.

18. Hammer a nail set or awl to make an indentation at each of the four marks.

19. Attach the flange with ¹/₂" countersink head wood screws.

20. Prime, paint, and decorate your box. This one was painted with bright yellow and orange enamel. Pre-painted wood butterfly and flower appliqués purchased from a craft store were adhered with waterproof carpenter's glue. To install the box, use a hammer to pound the pipe about 8" to 12" into the ground, and then screw the box flange onto the pipe.

Wind Chimes Template

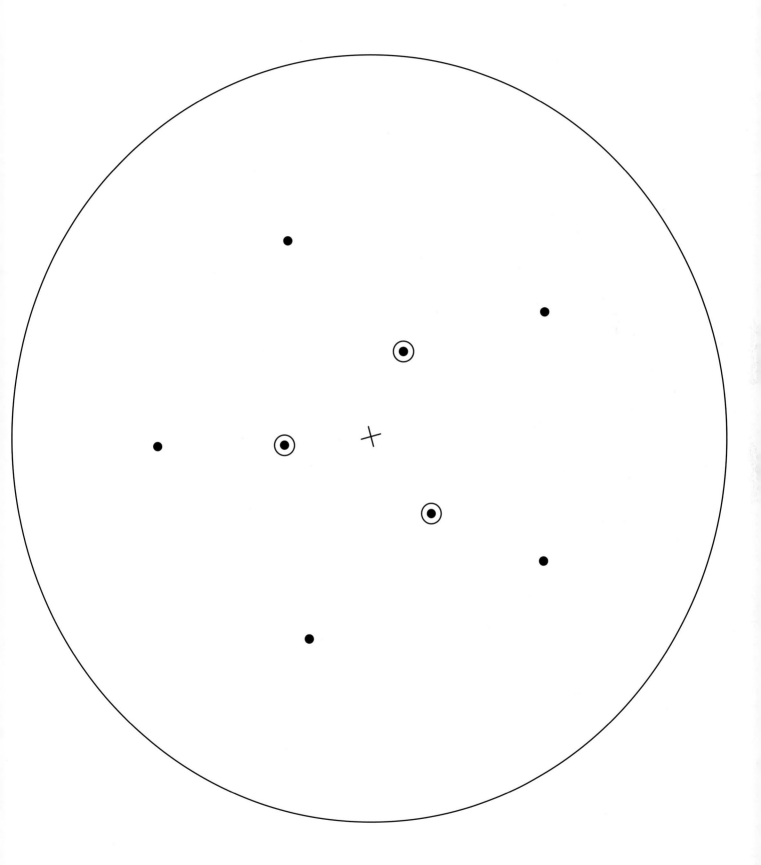

Clock Face Template

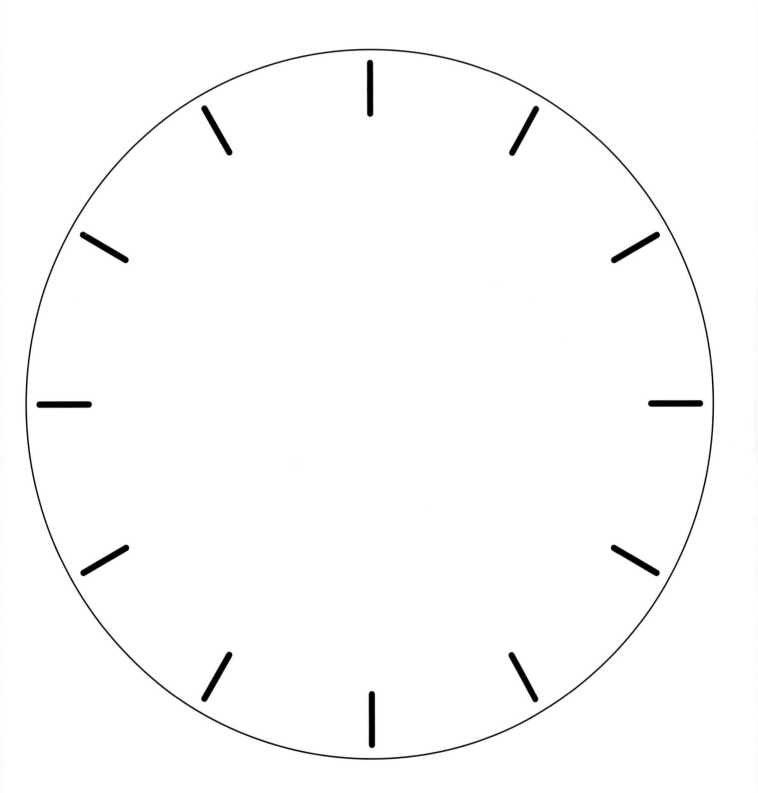

Acknowledgments

My heartfelt gratitude goes to my husband and extraordinary craftsman, Leon Letcavage, who built the bird, butterfly, and bee projects for this book. He taught me everything I know about woodworking, and was always there to answer questions and lend a helping hand on these craft projects. I am also grateful to have had such a skilled photographer in Alan Wycheck, whose patience is only surpassed by his great artistic talent. Thanks, too, to family members and friends who were continual sources of support, inspiration, and crafty ideas. Lastly, I am indebted to editor Mark Allison and his staff at Stackpole Books—the finest publisher of instructional books in the marketplace—for their vast expertise, and for giving me the opportunity to productively spend time making crafts for the garden and writing to tell about it.

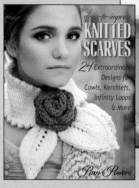

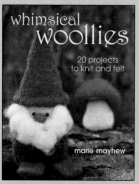